THE
Semantic Organizer
APPROACH
TO
WRITING AND READING
INSTRUCTION

Robert S. Pehrsson
Idaho State University

H. Alan Robinson
Hofstra University

AN ASPEN PUBLICATION®
Aspen Systems Corporation

1985

Rockville, Maryland
Royal Tunbridge Wells

Library of Congress Cataloging in Publication Data

Pehrsson, Robert S.
The semantic organizer approach to writing and reading instruction.

"An Aspen publication."
Includes bibliographies and index.
1. Language arts. 2. English language — Semantics —
Graphic methods. 3. English language — Semantics —
Study and teaching. I. Robinson, H. Alan, 1921- II. Title.
LBI576.P36 1985   372.6   85-15777
ISBN: 0-89443-866-2

Editorial Services: Martha Sasser

Library of Congress Catalog Card Number: 85-15777
ISBN: 0-89443-866-2

Printed in the United States of America

1 2 3 4 5

Table of Contents

Preface

The focus in this book is on helping learners capitalize on their cognitive strengths as they cope with reading and writing tasks. The semantic organizer approach is directed toward those teachers who share our basic assumption that most children need instruction in organizing ideas as a base for reading and writing. We are not providing a program or a method. Semantic organizers are tools that serve specific purposes and can be integrated into any reading and writing program.

Semantic organizers are valuable tools as preorganizers for writing and reading and as postorganizers. As preorganizers for reading, they help pupils understand major relationships in the reading assignment; when used as reading postorganizers they help to develop comprehension and retention strategies. As preorganizers for writing, semantic organizers assist pupils in planning major relationships and free them from worrying about syntax initially.

We believe in Donald Graves' work in writing and the Goodmans' in reading: Rich environments should be mobilized for allowing children to read and write on topics of interest to them. We also believe, however, that many children need much assistance in organizing their prior and present knowledge as they approach reading and writing tasks. Such help is especially needed when the school curriculum imposes content and tasks on pupils on which they have little background. We think that the best learning might take place if the curriculum did not ''impose''; it does, however, for many valid reasons, and the teacher must provide direction and structure. The sequence of semantic organizers in this book begins with tight control by the teacher and gradually places the responsibility on the learner.

This volume is intended for elementary and junior high school teachers who are endeavoring to teach and improve the reading strategies of pupils in classrooms across the curriculum. We first introduce semantic organizers as simple action tools suitable for kindergarten and/or grade one, as well as for older children in resource rooms. We then develop a variety of kinds of semantic organizers across the grades.

Although we have indicated grade levels for many of our specific examples, we do not, however, assign specific grade levels to the types of semantic organizers; ours is not a reading or writing program with a given sequence. Teachers must decide which organizers will be most useful for which students, at what time, and for what tasks.

The approach is primarily for those learners who need help in organizing ideas as they undertake writing and reading tasks. Semantic organizers have been used successfully in TESL (Teaching English as a Second Language) programs and in bilingual settings as well as with language disabled youngsters. We have also been pleased with the results when we have worked with high school and college students. As indicated, however, this book is directed specifically toward elementary, middle school, and junior high school teachers.

The volume begins with an introduction, or preorganizer, that acts as an overview. It then is organized in two parts: Part I: Underpinnings for Semantic Organizers (four brief chapters that provide the background for the specific strategies); Part II: Strategies for the Semantic Organizer Approach (nine chapters that spell out our developmental strategies for teaching reading and writing through the semantic organizer approach).

We are extremely grateful to the many learners from nursery school through university levels who have helped us develop, practice, assess, and modify the strategies presented here. We also are deeply grateful to the teachers at all levels, in a wide variety of teaching situations, for their cooperation, their insights, and their active assistance. We hope we have been as successful in putting these ideas and strategies in print as they have proved to be in practice.

Robert S. Pehrsson, Ed.D.
Idaho State University
Pocatello, Idaho

H. Alan Robinson, Ed.D.
Hofstra University
Hempstead, N.Y.

Introduction

Many approaches have been developed for teaching reading and a limited number have been spelled out for teaching writing. However, few have attempted to teach reading/writing strategies together. The authors treat reading and writing as closely connected processes in unfolding the semantic organizer approach described and demonstrated in this volume.

In all probability this book could not have been written too many years ago. It is only within recent years that the explosion of knowledge in the areas of language acquisition and language development has helped theoreticians as well as practitioners synthesize important notions about cognition and language. Years ago, a number of theories on language acquisition were based on superficial understandings of how language works. Today, although there still is much to learn, understanding of language acquisition and development seems to be growing; useful applications can be drawn from that emerging knowledge.

One important outcome is the movement away from a medical model of diagnosis and treatment. Users of that model search for the problem, then organize treatment for it. In looking at learners today, even those who are considered to be learning disabled, the tendency is to assess strengths as well as needs, then to set up programs that will capitalize on the strengths. All learners have cognitive or thinking-knowledge strengths. This notion forms the base as well as the continuing format for the authors' program: the semantic organizer approach presented in this book.

The theoretical underpinnings for the program explicated in Part I (Chapters 1 through 4) grow out of language acquisition understandings as well as linguistic theories that are relatively new and exciting. They also are based on the schema theory largely developed by Jean Piaget. The authors demonstrate how these theories are interrelated and how they form a foundation for applications in teaching.

Part II (Chapters 5 through 13) presents the practical applications the authors have developed in classroom settings. This part details the semantic organizer approach that can be begun with 4- and 5-year-olds and developed throughout the grades. Teachers will need to extend and apply these practical applications to their own particular situations, students, and content. Some teachers who have used the semantic organizer approach speak of it as an equalizer. It seems to help especially youngsters who have not internalized an organizational system that underlies their assimilation and accommodation of new information. Successful youngsters seem to have such an internalized organizational system.

Chapter 5 stresses the first two semantic organizers—realia and picture organizers—that help young learners, as well as older ones who have problems, begin to organize their cognitive strengths for reading and writing tasks. Chapter 6 deals with verb organizers that help to make the transition from readiness to coping with reading and writing.

Noun organizers are introduced in Chapter 7 as tools for improving reading and writing at a relatively simple level. The concept organizers in Chapter 8, with their focus on major and supporting ideas, link cognitive strengths to linguistic strengths. In Chapter 9 the episodic organizers stress sequential and chronological thinking patterns and help readers and writers become more successful with reading and writing in the content areas. Chapter 10 contains suggestions for moving away at times, in writing, from semantic organizers in order to encourage and nurture spontaneous creative writing.

Chapter 11 returns to semantic organizers and deals with the important notions of how to "correct" students in reading and writing. The suggestions emphasize selective editing and language expansion. In Chapter 12 organizers are discussed and demonstrated as tools for more mature thinking and for study strategies. Chapter 13 focuses on aids to the teacher for the use of semantic organizers in planning and executing lessons.

In writing the book, it appeared logical to develop the theoretical underpinnings, then move on to practice; hence, the book begins with the first four chapters related to theory. However, some readers may want to start with Chapter 5 and cover the chapters on strategies, then turn to Chapters 1–4 to ascertain the theoretical underpinnings.

The strategies throughout are based on and emphasize meaning. No language drills are provided. Strategies are based on the natural extension of children's thought and language. Thought processes form the base for the semantic organizer approach; the underlying philosophy is a focus on learners' strengths.

Part I

Underpinnings for Semantic Organizers

Chapter 1

Proximity and Reading/ Writing Strategies

The ideas discussed in this chapter, as well as in Chapters 2, 3, and 4, serve as vital underpinnings for this approach to the teaching of reading and writing. In this chapter, the concept of proximity (closeness of organized ideas shared by readers and writers) is developed and related to reading and writing strategies.

PROXIMITY

Reading and writing are closely related processes that reflect the organization of ideas in the minds of readers and writers. The degree to which readers and writers have similar ideas, organized in similar ways, is crucial to the success or failure of communication. This degree of "proximity" also influences the strategies used by writers and readers.

Successful readers possess or develop as much background related to writers' presentations as possible. The more the similarity, the easier it is for readers to comprehend authors' messages. In like manner, successful writers try to anticipate readers' backgrounds and attempt to bridge gaps, narrowing differences when necessary. Both readers and writers draw from their own organized and personal backgrounds. Both make use of prior information derived from their own cultures, internalized experiences, language, and interests. Hence, proximity (the degree of match between reader and writer) is dependent upon four interrelated factors: cultural, cognitive, linguistic, and affective.

Cultural

"Knowledge . . . is conditioned by culture. Therefore, a person's culture is a principal determiner of what he or she can come to know."[1]

What people think about, talk about, and feel about both themselves and others and the surrounding world is determined to a large extent by their culture. Readers and writers may have difficulties communicating if their cultures differ widely. Teachers need to make every effort to understand the cultural backgrounds of their students in order to help them make contact with the writers whose books are being used for instruction.

Understanding and discussing differences and similarities lead to increased cultural proximity. Intensive and extensive interactions among cultures, guided carefully by the teacher, help students broaden their backgrounds and approach reading and writing with heightened insights. Brainstorming and preorganizing for writing and reading tasks help students with diverse cultural backgrounds develop greater cultural proximity as they interact with an author or try to present their written ideas to an audience.

In all probability, culture is the most influential force in everyone's life. It certainly is the most significant of the proximity factors for it has an overriding effect on cognition, language, and emotions.

Cognitive

Cognitive proximity refers to the degree of match between the thinking and organized knowledge of the reader and the writer. The more common knowledge they share, the greater the likelihood of cognitive proximity.

Teachers need to help students develop and/or mobilize knowledge for a given reading or writing task. Such development and mobilization need to be related to the organization of ideas as presented by an author or as anticipated by those who plan to read what a student has written.

For instance, a text may be organized to demonstrate a cause-effect relationship; if the reader fails to organize in the same way as the author, the degree of proximity will be slight and comprehension will be faulty. Or, a text may be organized in such a way that information is related to a topic in factual form but the reader organizes in story form. For example, if an author writes an expository passage about the characteristics of turtles but the reader interprets it as a sequential story on turtles, there obviously is a distinct failure of communication; much of what the writer had hoped to share with the reader may be lost.

Linguistic

Linguistic proximity is the degree of match between the words used by the writer and those used by the reader. It is a rather natural consideration when people use oral language. They use different syntactic structures and vocabulary when they explain something to a child as compared with what they say to adults. The degree of linguistic proximity between reader and writer—and writer and reader—is of equal or even greater importance. If the reader has difficulty with vocabulary, is unfamiliar with syntactic structures, and cannot relate words to one another in meaningful ways as intended by the author, comprehension suffers. Similarly, as a writer, the student must learn to adapt language to the intended audience if communication is the desired outcome.

A number of linguistic subtleties in written discourse have an effect on proximity. Readers and writers need to understand how words and larger units of meaning interrelate not only within sentences but also among sentences within an organized piece of writing. For example, a reader must be aware of certain linguistic cues in order to understand relationships among the following sentences:

Many people smoke cigarettes. Unfortunately, that can damage their lungs as well as the lungs of innocent people around them for they breathe in the same toxic smoke. Those who do so may be subject to serious lung diseases.

Each of the three sentences can stand the traditional test of a complete idea, with subject and predicate, that stands on its own. In reality, however, the second and third sentences make sense only if related to the first, and even so there is ambiguity. Obviously, each sentence cannot stand on its own—at least semantically. The word "that" in the second sentence and "do so" in the third are called cohesive ties by Halliday and Hasan; they guide the reader in making connections among sentences.[2] Readers are called upon to understand the relationship between referent and antecedent just as writers need to clarify the relationship.

Teachers need to help learners become more aware of some of the language units they will encounter in their reading and use in their own writing. Increased linguistic proximity enhances reading and writing. In addition, as teachers assist students to stretch linguistically, they will be increasing both cultural and cognitive proximity.

Affective

Affective proximity is the degree of interest in a subject shared by reader and writer. In reading, it refers to the amount of interest and feeling the reader shares with the writer about the topic and the development of the story or the information presented. In writing, it refers to the writer's awareness in presenting material of interest to an audience and in organizing it to appeal to that interest.

Teachers should make every attempt, when dealing with instructional material, to interest or involve students in the reading task. At times that attempt is undermined by poorly written and poorly organized text as well as by curriculum demands that do not make contact with the pupils. Teachers then have a challenging job indeed, to help students become more knowledgeable about topics before the reading so they approach the task with a little more feeling of involvement.

In writing, teachers need to help learners make their writing as interesting as possible by providing opportunities to become involved in writing tasks that make contact with real audiences with whom the writers want to communicate. Too often young writers merely fulfill assignments rather than using writing as an important communication tool. Once they realize that they write not just to hand something in to the teacher but because they have something they want to communicate, involvement and interest are evident and assured.

STRATEGIES

Reading

Reading is a process (or perhaps a set of processes) by which people generate and organize their memories related to a topic, allow their thinking to be guided externally, assimilate new ideas, accommodate old ones, and then reorganize. Reading begins and ends with meaning.

Reading is constructive.[3] Individuals construct and reconstruct their organization of ideas before reading, then reconstruct again based upon what they know as a result of reading. Reading also is a selective behavior.[4] The reader selects from text what appears to be important information and disregards what seems to be less important. What is of great importance is the interaction between reader and writer, resulting in an interpretation of the writer's message.

Three major strategies are involved in reading: (1) semantic, (2) syntactic, and (3) phonographological. Semantic strategies make use of meaning in the head of the reader as well as the representation of meaning in the text. Syntactic strategies involve the language competence of the reader in relation to the syntactic structures—paragraphs, sentences, other clauses and phrases—in the text. Phonographological strategies call on the reader's ability to make use of phoneme-grapheme relationships (sounds and their visual representations) in figuring out words, phrases, and other meaning units. (Some instructors emphasize phonographological strategies at the expense of the others. Luckily for deaf students these are not the only strategies. Deaf youngsters, and many learning disabled pupils with auditory processing problems, learn to read through the other two strategies and, in this way, compensate for their handicap.)

Different theorists and researchers seem to place different emphases on specific sets of strategies. This is evident in inspecting the reading models of three commonly cited theorists—Gough,[5] Goodman,[6] and Rumelhart.[7] The major differences among these three representatives of points of view may be observed in their explanations of (1) what initiates the reading, (2) how readers process information, and (3) how readers organize information.

According to Gough, reading starts with the print on the page. The process begins when the reader looks at each letter, produces an equivalent phoneme (sound) for each grapheme (written symbol that represents a phoneme), synthesizes these into words, and eventually deals with the syntactic structures (sentences, etc.) and meaning intended by the writer. Based on Gough's model, readers employ strategies in the following order: (a) visual (look at print), (b) auditory (ascertain sounds), (c) syntactic (synthesize words into sentences), and (d) semantic (understand words, sentences, and paragraphs). In Gough's view, accuracy of visual and auditory strategies is of prime importance based on the assumption that memory is organized as abstract phonemes. To arrive at meaning the reader must go through a language process that depends largely on sound equivalents for words.

In contrast, Goodman takes the view that reading begins with an hypothesis or prediction about the meaning of what is to be read. Readers make initial use of their prior knowledge and language competence. They search the page in order to confirm, refine, or reject predicted meaning and language. Based on Goodman's view, readers use strategies in the following order: (a) semantic (predict meaning), (b) syntactic (generate anticipated language possibilities to structure anticipated meaning), and (c) visual in combination with auditory (confirm expectations). Goodman's constant focus is on meaning. The reader does not need to look at or pronounce every letter or word to get to meaning. The reader samples and selects from the text only the most useful information with the intent of confirming expectations.

Rumelhart suggests that the reading process may be initiated either by the print or by the reader's expectations. The reader makes use of whatever strategies are needed at the time. Based on Rumelhart's model, the reader may place emphasis on semantic/syntactic strategies but when necessary will emphasize visual/auditory strategies. Under any conditions, in Rumelhart's model, the reader attempts to fit information into schemata (networks of interrelated concepts in the mind) and, to do so, uses whatever strategies are needed in whatever order they are required.

Regardless of the model, there is general agreement that comprehension is the goal of reading. The authors of this book tend to agree with Goodman and Rumelhart that reading is an interactive process that involves meaning from start to finish. Rumelhart's model seems particularly logical in regard to the use of top–down (beginning with prior organized information in the head of the reader) or bottom–up (beginning with the printed or written symbols) strategies when applicable.

Good readers do seem to shift gears. When they find it difficult to understand what they are reading, they tend to make greater use of the graphic information, to read more slowly, and even to bring language to the surface by reading orally. In a sense they need to use a lower gear and more energy when the material is not highly predictable. However, it would be highly inefficient to attend to individual words if reading is easy and predictable. When the reader can easily approximate the writer's ideas and language through anticipation, the distance is minimal and fewer cues on the page are necessary; a "higher gear," emphasizing semantic/syntactic strategies, should be employed. Such a top–down approach usually is the most efficient route to effective communication.

Writing

Writing usually begins with some type of brainstorming of ideas to help us know what we know about a topic. We then turn to representing ideas in some organized form so they can be interpreted by a reader. A writer develops "maps," one before the actual putting of connected thoughts on paper, then one in written form for the reader. The written or printed map contains linguistic cues and content represented by words, word order, inflected word endings, punctuation, sentences, paragraphs, etc.

Before the reader's map is organized, the writer needs to do a number of things (whether using pen, pencil, typewriter, or word processor). After brainstorming ideas, an effective writer develops a purpose for writing to a targeted audience. Next, the writer organizes those ideas and decides on an organizational format. Some type of outline or organizer is helpful at this point. After arranging and rearranging ideas in logical ways, the writing begins. The primary emphasis should be on clarifying the message for the intended audience. A number of revisions might take place at this point, all directed toward clarification of meaning. Gradually, still with the audience in mind, concerns about vocabulary, spelling, grammar, sentence complexity, and paragraph organization arise.

The next steps usually are reading and rereading with the intent of further revising as well as editing. Here the writer takes the place of the reader and attempts to refine ideas and language. Always anticipating the reader's background, the writer, like the reader, needs to adapt strategies appropriately related to the anticipated proximity between writer and reader.

Although this description of the writing process may seem linear and prescribed, it is not intended to be so. It describes the ingredients in a process that may be approached in such steps. Most of the time such steps are present but many writers may alter the order. In addition, the writing process probably never follows such a rigid sequence. Flower and Hayes speak of:

1. planning, in which the writer sets goals and plans the content of a paper
2. translating, in which plans and knowledge are expressed in a written text
3. reviewing, in which the results of planning and translating are tested.[8]

Within this framework, the writer may make recurrent movements since plans may change in the translating or reviewing, or the reviewing might necessitate changes in the translating, etc.

At any rate, the purpose of writing is to represent meanings so they may be interpreted by a reader. The transmittal of clear meaning is the primary goal. Sometimes, depending on the nature and purpose of a piece of writing, nonstandard spelling, inappropriate grammar, and poor handwriting impede communication. Learners need to be helped to develop strategies for editing within the meaningful contexts of their written discourse. Isolated spelling and grammar lessons help little in developing effective writers.

Inter-relationships

The common practice of teaching reading during one period of the day and writing in another (if at all) hinders the development of both. Classroom practices and reading lab procedures that concentrate on ''reading skills'' and use minimal writing activities for filling in short answers in workbooks are counterproductive for learners. There is a strong relationship between reading and writing; the development of writing has a positive influence on reading, and vice versa, if they are learned and taught in concert. For young children who are learning to read, it is important that they learn to write.[9] By learning reading and writing as an integrated activity, they are more able to transfer strategies from one task to another.

(Part II introduces the authors' semantic organizer approach, which emphasizes many kinds of relationships. It begins with the amalgamation of thinking and organizing skills plus oral language. It progresses to using an integration of reading/writing strategies for both reading and writing tasks.)

ROLES OF SEMANTIC ORGANIZERS

As indicated in the preface, the semantic organizer approach to reading and writing instruction is not a program. Semantic organizers are *tools* for helping readers preorganize for reading, and sometimes for postorganizing their ideas after interacting with an author. They are tools for helping writers brainstorm and organize their ideas in what Temple, Nathan, and Burris describe as the stage of composing called rehearsal (term borrowed from Murray).

> Rehearsing is the stage in which writers discover what they have to say. In the rehearsing stage, the writer considers the widest range of ideas that might possibly be written about. Sometimes teachers encourage rehearsing by means of brainstorming sessions, in which children think up and write down as many details as they can about a person, a place or an event which is meaningful to them.[10]

In the semantic organizer approach to writing, especially for children having difficulty getting started as writers or when children are not generating their own original stories but have classroom writing tasks to accomplish, we first control the range of ideas that might be used in a composition. Then, as children become adept at organizing and feel comfortable about writing, we introduce organizers which allow them as much freedom in brainstorming and organizing ideas as they would like.

CONCLUSION

Reading and writing are closely related tasks that should not be taught apart from one another. Readers and writers need to have a close relationship if communication is to take place. That relationship, degree of proximity, is composed of four major factors: cultural, cognitive, linguistic, and affective. Writing and reading success depends on close proximity as well as the organization of ideas. Children need help in organizing ideas, particularly for tasks assigned by the teacher. An important way of helping youngsters realize and capitalize on the relationships between authors and readers is to develop reading and writing instruction as an integrated activity.

NOTES

1. Richard C. Anderson, "Some Reflections on the Acquisition of Knowledge," *Educational Researcher* 13, no. 9 (November 1984): 8.
2. Michael A.K. Halliday and Ruqaiya Hasan, *Cohesion in English* (London: Longmans, Ltd., 1976).
3. Robert J. Tierney, Connie Bridge, and Mary Jane Cera, "The Discourse Processing Operations of Children," *Reading Research Quarterly* 14, no. 4 (1978–79): 539–73.
4. Kenneth S. Goodman, "Behind the Eye: What Happens in Reading," in *Reading Process and Program,* ed. Kenneth S. Goodman and Olive S. Niles (Urbana, Ill.: National Council of Teachers of English, 1970), 3–38.
5. Philip B. Gough, "One Second of Reading," in *Language by Ear and by Eye,* ed. J.F. Kavanagh and I.G. Mattingly (Cambridge, Mass.: The MIT Press, 1972), 331–58.
6. Kenneth S. Goodman, "Reading: A Psycholinguistic Guessing Game," in *Theoretical Models and Processes of Reading,* 2nd ed., ed. Harry Singer and Robert B. Ruddell (Newark, Del.: International Reading Association, 1976).
7. David E. Rumelhart, "Toward an Interactive Model of Reading," in *Attention and Performance VI,* ed. Stanislav Dornic (New York: Halsted Press Division of John Wiley & Sons, Inc., 1977).
8. Linda Flower and John R. Hayes, "Plans That Guide the Composing Process," in *Writing: The Nature, Development, and Teaching of Written Composition; Vol. 2, Writing: Process, Development and Communication,* ed. Carl H. Frederikson and Joseph F. Dominic (Hillsdale, N.J.: Lawrence Erlbaum Associates, Inc., 1981), 41.
9. Leonard Sealey, Nancy Sealey, and Marcia Millmore, *Children's Writing* (Newark, Del.: International Reading Association, 1979), 7.
10. Charles A. Temple, Ruth G. Nathan, and Nancy A. Burris, *The Beginnings of Writing* (Boston: Allyn and Bacon, Inc., 1982), 187.

Chapter 2

The Cognitive Underpinnings

Chapters 2 and 3 explain the cognitive and linguistic constructs, the roots of the semantic organizer approach presented in Part II. This chapter discusses the cognitive or thought processes, Chapter 3 the linguistic or language processes. The separation into two chapters is done purely for ease in presentation; in reality, it is almost impossible to separate the obvious interactions of thought and language.

COGNITIVE ORGANIZATION

Of all the things they do best, young people remember and think about their own personal experiences. To do this thinking and remembering, they must organize their ideas. Organization is the key to memory.[1]

Cognitive Strengths

Because each individual has had different life experiences and/or different interpretations of those experiences, each categorizes world views somewhat differently. As distinct and personal as this organization may be, it nevertheless is organization. All learners have this strength, some perhaps more than others, to store in memory organized networks of their experiences. In a given culture or subculture, groups of individuals have some similar organizational structures or schemata stored away.

In the beginning developmental stages of growth, it probably is true that thought structures language.[2] Later, however, language plays an important role in structuring thought.[3] The early cognitive structures of an infant are ready for language, and language at that point is highly contagious. If language is not "caught" at this critical period, then these language-ready structures seem to begin to shut down. Some children who do not have a strong experiential base—a multitude of in-depth schemata—may develop weaknesses in language, especially in the realm of vocabulary development. They may find some linguistic doors shutting.

But all is not lost. They still have potential cognitive strengths and the intervention of the important adult—the teacher—is significant. With appropriate guidance and a sequential development of cognitive-linguistic strategies, such children can be helped.

Developmental Stages

Human beings are in a constant state of trying to make sense out of their worlds. Each is constructing hypotheses, generating knowledge, anticipating what will happen next, and making inferences about what should be but is not. Each attempts to understand how things, people, and events interact. The ultimate, and perhaps innate, aim is that people organize their worlds into sensible wholes. This sense of a together world is satisfying and important; it provides the cognitive system with a sense of equilibrium. However, this sensible whole goes through continual change as this equilibrium is challenged by conflicting information. The built-in mechanism that copes with change consists of schemata—the basic organizational structures that assimilate (take in) information about the world, then change to accommodate the new information.

Piaget postulates developmental stages for such changes.[4] Initially, even infants organize their sense of the world, primarily with the aid of sensory perceptions and reflexes, and through physical relationships. As children mature, they can appreciate the relations that exist among a series of actions. They develop the significant understanding that objects can be rearranged yet remain the same quantity, that a material can be changed without affecting the mass, and that a scene can be viewed from a different perspective yet remain the same. These understandings probably are of vital importance to reading and writing since they permit recognition and shaping of diverse structures.

According to Piaget, the stage of formal operations, a more mature way of viewing the world, is initiated in early adolescence. Youths, in addition to reasoning through actions and primitive symbol systems, now can also figure out the implications related to a set of propositions. Piaget emphasizes that although logic and hypothesis testing underlie each stage, at the formal operations stage learners can test out a set of propositions and revise them as a result of experimentation. This stage carries adolescents into adult life ready to grow and adapt to an ever-changing environment. The times Piaget allots to his stages may fluctuate a little among individuals and cultures, but his contribution of a sequence of stages makes clear that testing and changing of schemata must take place or no real intellectual growth can occur.

Trial and error are necessary for growth. Most likely, those who do not try for fear of error will fail to grow cognitively as well. This notion has major implications for teaching reading and writing, because if youngsters are afraid to make mistakes, they will fail to learn. Teachers must develop the attitude themselves and among their students that mistakes are important ways of learning and that perhaps the biggest error of all is not to learn from mistakes.

Another application of Piaget's concepts, important to reading and writing, is that individuals learn from action. New schemata develop initially through direct interactions with the world. Later, after basic schemata have been developed, symbolic processes that probably are still rooted in internalized actions become useful for thinking. In teaching reading/writing, teachers must be sure that students are actively involved in the construction of, and interaction with, written language. The semantic organizer approach used here is dedicated to that proposition.

ORGANIZA-TIONAL STRATEGIES

Schemata Development

Organizational strategies ultimately are governed by schemata, those data structures that represent the generic networks of concepts stored in memory.[5] Schemata activate similar behaviors under similar sets of circumstances and thus help people know how to behave in a variety of different but similar circumstances. For example, individuals as youngsters probably learned how to act around guests in a general sense based on experiences with previous guests as well as admonitions and reminders from parents. Schemata also help people understand differences among objects, people, and events. For instance, they may develop two schemata for eating because they realize that these call for different sets of behaviors in different contexts—such as eating at a barbecue and dining in a fancy restaurant.

A schema is generalizable and useful in another but similar action or operation.[6] Individuals may comprehend a story better if they have had experiences similar to those of the main character. They may be able to write a story that will involve their readers if they are aware of the readers' experiential backgrounds.

Schemata are like the file systems for memories; improperly filed memories may never be found. Learners who have problems remembering something may have failed to file information in an appropriate schema. The problem usually is not poor memory but poor organization at the time of learning.

Patterns

Bruner emphasizes that much of learning and problem solving involves the task of identifying regularities.[7] Networks of information within schemata seem organized mainly in two regular ways: sequential and whole/parts. Such patterns occur over and over again in people's heads (often in concert or in tandem) and, of course, in text. The pupil not only must use these organizational patterns in storing and retrieving information but also must learn to spot them in the material being read and to use them in the material being written.

Sequence is order of events or actions; usually, one event or action triggers the next. Some goal is achieved when the sequence is completed—the steps in getting ready for school, the steps in blowing glass, the events resulting in a presidential inauguration. By observing the steps—and often the cause-effect relationships within them—individuals learn to anticipate outcomes and effects from their own behavior and from events in general. Emphasizing this type of sequential or episodic organization, Pearson and Johnson suggest that knowledge is organized schematically around "typical scenarios or scripts."[8]

Episodes or sequences involve change. The other way information is organized—whole/parts—ignores change and focuses on relationships of the parts to the whole. Much teaching is done in this way and most expository textbooks highlight whole/parts (sometimes referred to as superordinate/subordinate) in their overall organization of ideas, with parts devoted to sequence. For example, categorizing various states in the United States into their regions (Northwest, Middle Atlantic, etc.) would call up the superordinate (the name of each region) and the subordinate (the states listed under each region). Episodes or sequences (order of the states) would be unnecessary.

(The semantic organizer approach in Part II stresses relationships of the parts to the whole and sequential patterns.)

Teaching Schemata

When information is presented to learners, it should be connected, well-organized, in-depth information. At the same time, learners should be helped to organize and reorganize information for improved retention during and after reading[9] and for effective writing.

As suggested earlier, the reading and writing processes are closely related. The ability to organize schemata is at the root of both. All children can organize, but it is how they organize in relation to reading and writing that counts. In written language a topic and related sentences (whole/parts) represent an author's cognitive organization. The author's organization (as indicated in Chapter 1) must be approximated by a reader in order to comprehend the intended meaning. A writer must be able to generalize a topic and connect ideas to it logically.

Some difficulties learners encounter appear to be linked to the development of inefficient schemata. Teachers need to be especially tuned to the need to help pupils develop effective schemata for given tasks. Retention and meaningfulness of new learning are influenced strongly by whether or not the learner has assimilated information into an organizational pattern (schema) or has attempted to amass a string of isolated bits. Nothing (vocabulary words, facts, etc.) should be taught or learned in isolation. "Higher levels of thinking" depend on basic organizational categories and patterns of categories that can be applied again and again in related situations.

According to Dewey, it makes all the difference whether the acquisition of new information is treated as an end in itself or as an integral part of the training of thought.[10] The training of thought involves a continual search for organizational patterns in reality and expanding organizational patterns in the mind through categorizing, generalizing, inferring, anticipating, and constantly seeking to go beyond the literal level of the information given.[11] Bruner suggests that it is only by imparting generic codes (schemata) that education in the broad range of human knowledge is made possible. Education does best to aim at generic codes to train students to transfer learning, to go beyond the information given, and to anticipate events and interrelationships based on the probable reconstruction of the organizational pattern at hand.

NEURO-LOGICAL INSIGHTS

The human brain is divided into hemispheres that are connected predominantly by a bundle of about 200 million nerve fibers called the corpus callosum. The hemispheres function differently. In most individuals the left hemisphere is responsible for language-related tasks, the right hemisphere for, among other things, spatial relationships and creativity.[12]

There are underlying reasons why the left hemisphere is better equipped to process language and the right to process spatial relationships: the two hemispheres have different information processing styles, parts-to-whole vs. whole-to-parts. The left hemisphere deals with parts-to-whole information, and language usually is presented in this way, especially in school. In contrast, the whole-to-parts processing of the right hemisphere is most suitable for dealing with two- and three-dimensional forms on the basis of common geometrical features[13] and in perceiving whole-part relationships when presented as line drawings.[14]

There is a strong possibility that schools have done a disservice to many youngsters who have greater strengths in their right rather than their left. Bogen suggests that teaching has neglected, even starved, the right hemisphere and ignored its potential strengths that can be developed.[15] For example, boys, who seem to have greater problems learning to read and write than do girls, tend to lateralize much earlier than girls. This means that "girls . . . seem to be able to use either hemisphere equally well for language and visuospatial processing, at least until the age of 14."[16] In general, women tend to be more bilateral than men, which means that women have a better ability to process both verbal and nonverbal information in both hemispheres.

It is very likely, then, that many learners—especially boys—have strengths that the schools have not tapped well. Right-brain strengths can be developed when practitioners teach whole to parts at least with as much zeal as when they teach parts to whole. A number of youngsters probably would learn better if the teaching strategies used involved both right and left hemispheres. Students then could draw upon whichever hemisphere was needed to accomplish a given task or, more important, could use an integration of both hemispheres for the task.

The teaching of reading and writing should incorporate right-brain, visuospatial relationships. Texts—the representation of ideas through words, sentences, and paragraphs—can be transformed and recoded as visual-spatial relationships that maintain the original basic representation of meaning. (Part II emphasizes the transforming of ideas into semantic organizers that are visuospatial representations along with language. Right-brain processing is highlighted, along with left-brain processing.)

CONCLUSION

Any child remotely ready to read and write is able to organize information. Schemata are the basic structures for accomplishing this organization; they are somewhat like networks and filing systems, but they are extremely dynamic. Schemata are developed principally by trial and error and, most importantly, through action. They are organized, basically, in two ways: relationships of parts to whole, and sequential order.

Transfer of learning is the ability to apply information learned in one situation to other situations. In fact, that's what learning is all about. Schemata are the structures that permit such transfer of learning. The semantic organizer approach directs learning to schemata and to right-brain as well as left-brain organizing.

NOTES

1. Jerome Bruner and Jacqueline J. Goodnow, "After John Dewey, What?" in *On Knowing* (New York: Atheneum Publishers, 1965).

2. Jean Piaget, *The Language and Thought of the Child* (New York: Meridian Books, 1955).

3. Lev Vygotsky, *Thought and Language* (Cambridge, Mass.: The MIT Press, 1962).

4. Piaget, *Language and Thought.*

5. David E. Rumelhart, "Schemata: The Building Blocks of Cognition," in *Comprehension and Teaching: Research Reviews,* ed. John T. Guthrie (Newark, Del.: International Reading Assocation, 1981).

6. Jean Piaget, *On the Development of Memory and Identity* (Barre, Mass.: Clark University Press, 1968).

7. Jerome Bruner, *Beyond the Information Given* (New York: W.W. Norton & Company, Inc., 1973).

8. P. David Pearson and Dale D. Johnson, *Teaching Reading Comprehension* (New York: Holt, Rinehart & Winston, 1978).

9. Barbara M. Taylor, "Children's Memory for Expository Text After Reading," *Reading Research Quarterly* 15, no. 3 (1980): 399–411.

10. John Dewey, *How Do We Think?* (New York: D.C. Heath & Co. 1933).

11. Bruner, *Beyond the Information Given.*

12. Sally P. Springer and Georg Deutsch, *Left Brain, Right Brain* (San Francisco: W.H. Freeman & Co., 1981).

13. L. Franco and R.W. Sperry, "Hemisphere Lateralization for Cognitive Processing of Geometry," *Neuropsychologia* 15 (1977): 7–114.

14. Robert D. Nebes, "Dominance of the Minor Hemisphere in Commissurotomized Man in a Test of Figure Unification," *Brain* 95 (1972): 633–38.

15. Joseph E. Bogen, "The Other Side of the Brain. VII: Some Educational Aspects of Hemispheric Specialization," *UCLA Educator* 17, no. 2 (Spring 1975): 24–32.

16. Richard Sinatra and Josephine Stahl-Gemake, *Using the Right Brain in the Language Arts* (Springfield, Ill.: Charles C Thomas, Publisher, 1983).

Chapter 3

The Linguistic Underpinnings

Chapter 2, on the cognitive underpinnings of the authors' teaching approach, presented theoretical notions to demonstrate how schemata and organizational patterns form strong bases for the acquisition and expansion of thinking and language. This chapter offers the linguistic underpinnings.

Language has content, form, and function. A writer organizes information and uses strategies to develop written language forms that function to communicate content. For the writer, content is first. Form is important, but only after content is clearly developed; then the writer may think about specific words, phrases, sentences, and paragraphs. At all times, of course, the writer is concerned about the major function of communication to an audience.

CONTENT, FORM, AND FUNCTION

Content has been called, by some, the meaning of a book.[1] But content is distinct from meaning. People carry meanings;[2] books carry content.

Content

In reading, the mind of the reader constructs textual content largely through the use of organizational patterns. Similarly, in writing, meanings are organized, then content is constructed as organizational patterns in graphic form. The content *represents*, in text, the ideas that the writer intended.

Oral language is composed of three forms: phonology, syntactic structures, and semantic relationships. Phonology is the sound system of language. Syntactic structures (syntax) are the ways words are ordered in phrases, sentences, and even larger units. Semantic relationships are the ways in which words relate meaningfully to one another within and among the sentences used in oral discourse. All of the forms interact continually; language cannot be used for adequate communication by using one or two of the forms in isolation. One of the major problems with ineffective

Form

17

instruction in reading and writing has been the isolated emphasis on phonology or syntax.

Sounds and
Symbols

Written language, of course, is closely related to oral; however, a major difference is the form of the coding system. Sound (phonology) is basic to oral language while written language is expressed in a graphological code, or in written symbols. The individual sounds of letters are called phonemes; the written letters are graphemes.

Graphemes are the smallest bits of information in written language. They do not normally represent meaning. Morphemes, on the other hand, do represent meaning. They are the smallest meaning-bearing units in a language system. Morphemes can be words that stand alone or parts of words. For example, the word "book" is a morpheme that stands on its own; it is called unbound. The word "books," however, is composed of two morphemes, "book" and "s." The "s" is a bound morpheme; it cannot stand alone, but it does have meaning since it refers to more than one. The rule system that governs how graphemes and morphemes work together to form words is known as orthography.

Syntax

Word order is of tremendous importance in English. Words placed in different orders will alter the meaning of a sentence, clause, or even a phrase. Subject, predicate, and object are significant syntactic structures. For example, word order makes all the difference in the meaning represented in the following two sentences: (1) The boy hit the ball. (2) The ball hit the boy.

Very young children seem to acquire a sense of syntax quickly and demonstrate syntactic awareness even when they can produce only two- or three-word utterances. For instance, one 2-year-old effectively used syntax to communicate with his older brother, who was hitting him. He said, "No hit me. Me hit." Then he hit his older brother. The difference between "hit me" and "me hit" was clearly understood because of the syntax and the nonverbal context, even though the objective form was used instead of the nominative in "Me hit."

Semantics

Semantic relationships among words have to do with the way in which meaning is represented in language; although syntax is of great importance, semantic relationships hold the key to the content. Obviously meanings are represented only partially by individual words. Understanding the meanings of isolated words is not the same as for words in combination with other words. For example, each of these individual words represents some degree of meaning:

house	trim
the	white
man	with
finished	the

But, of course, they do not represent the same meaning when related semantically to one another, as in "The man finished the house with white trim." Orthography and syntax are useful in uncovering the intended meaning in the sentence—meaning that is communicated by the semantic relationships among the words.

The sentence, "The man finished the house with white trim," may make sense to those with certain experiences related to house painting. To many readers it cannot stand on its own. This is not unusual. Many, if not most, sentences in normal contexts fail to make clear sense when isolated from a larger context. Indeed, the ability to comprehend the content of sentences often depends on semantic relationships not just within but among sentences.

Normally, ideas presented in written language are related in paragraph form. "There is no such thing as an isolated sentence in true linguistic behavior."[3] Teachers may note this for themselves by choosing any page from any book and reading a sentence at random. In most cases the sentence will beg for a larger context. Robinson suggests that "the basic unit for presenting a particular central thought or group of closely related ideas is the paragraph."[4] There are even times when the paragraph fails to represent a thought fully; sometimes an even larger context is required.

A major related point is that learners should begin instruction in reading and writing with natural language, not individual words or individual sentences. Meaning depends on the interactions of orthography, syntax, and semantic relationships among the sentences in a piece of written discourse.

Function

Language functions as a mapping system. Writers use language in order to present a map representing an organization of ideas that will approximate the organization of schemata in their minds as closely as possible. Readers, on the other hand, use language to direct the organization and reorganization of schemata in their minds as they attempt to approximate the authors' concepts.

Knowledge of the functions of individual words or groups of closely related words develops before learners acquire any in-depth understanding of overall content. Children know the use of words long before they can define them or realize that they have integral forms. For example, a young child does not know the definition of an object such as "chair" but certainly knows how to use both the chair and the word. In that sense, the function of language precedes form and content.

Although children know functions of individual words, those functions always are in a context. They learn words not in isolation but in functional, meaningful contexts. Hence, they learn faster when words are presented in rich, meaningful contexts.[5] In experiences with learning situations, the authors find that youngsters often become word-by-word readers if the emphasis, from the beginning, is not placed on how words relate to one another in written language.

Clark suggests that children build toward adult knowledge of word meanings by gradually adding features of information.[6] Initially, children "know" a word because they know one or two things about it in a specific and limited context. They frequently overgeneralize their knowledge of the word to other contexts, then slowly reduce that overgeneralization as they add more features of the word to their feature list. For example, a baby may learn that the animal barking and running around the highchair is a "dog." The major features the child may relate to are that the "dog" barks and runs fast. Actually, the child starts to develop a set of features about "dogs." The abstract representation of the child's feature list would be:

DOGS
bark   +
run fast   +

If the two features—bark and run fast—remain the only ones on the child's hypothetical list, it can be predicted that the youngster will call a cat a dog if the cat is running fast. If an adult, usually the parent, informs the child that the cat is not a dog, and the child hears the cat "meow," the child may add a negative to the "dog" feature list:

DOGS
bark   +
run fast   +
meow   −

The presence of an unclassified object can be uncomfortable for a child.[7] Thus, the child usually is motivated to revise a feature list or establish a new one with the name supplied by the adult added to the new experience:

CATS
meow   +
run fast   +
bark   −

Obviously, a youngster does not simply understand the meaning of a word by learning what an object is called. As Smith indicates, "Children do not need to be told interminably what a word is; they have to see what it is not."[8] In the development of feature lists in relation to words, "acquaintance with a wide variety of nonequivalent alternatives is everything."

SEMANTICS AND SYNTAX

Chomsky proposes that language is generated from a syntactic base that, in combination with the lexicon (vocabulary), determines the semantic interpretation of a sentence.[9] A growing number of theorists and researchers now suggest, however, that syntax is acquired only after semantic relations are established. Their arguments are important for purposes here because the approach described in this book is based on the notion that semantic relationships are primary and, in a sense, syntax is secondary. The authors' general developmental sequence and, indeed, the specific techniques at each stage, are based on the idea that meaning is represented as sets of semantic relationships in language first, with syntactic structures determined afterward.

Some theoretical views that have influenced this approach have been drawn from the research in early language acquisition. Brown emphasizes the importance of analyzing semantic intentions of children rather than the syntactic nature of their utterances.[10] Halliday calls grammatical options the realization of semantic ones. He suggests that a young child's "grammar" is semantic.[11,12] In the earliest stages of development, youngsters may not be using words alone to communicate; rather, through a combination of vocalized information, context, and nonverbal actions, they can get adults to interpret their intentions with relative accuracy. Semantic intentions precede syntax. Later, a two-word utterance such as "Mommy byebye" gets meaning across succinctly.

Bowerman points out that children are not seeking the means of expressing a grammatical relation such as subject-predicate but rather are trying to express semantic interactions such as an agent in relation to an action.[13] She adds that semantic concepts are more accessible than syntactic ones. It takes more effort for children to produce syntactic structures than to realize semantic relationships. After they have mastered some of the rudimentary semantic aspects of language, they turn to syntactic structuring. For one thing, mature syntax requires more words that need to be inserted appropriately into sentence structures; semantic relationships get more to the heart of basic relationships.

Bloom notes that syntax is not a prerequisite for a baby's apparent comprehension of spoken language.[14] There usually is enough redundancy in the total context for the child to understand the semantic intent with little or no regard for the syntactic constructions employed. In addition, mothers and fathers usually have little trouble understanding a child's nonstandard syntactic constructions because they make use of the semantic utterances in conjunction with their understanding of the child's needs and the context.

Halliday emphasizes the importance of context and situation in the analysis of each utterance.[15] He suggests the presence of a stratum in language, composed of "semantic networks," that is intermediate—between social system and grammatical system. Semantic networks "describe the range of alternative meanings available to the speaker in given social contexts and settings. . . ." These networks form a bridge between meaning and grammar. (The concept of semantic networks is basic to the practical applications to reading and writing in Part II. Semantic networks are in the brain; semantic organizers can be represented on paper.)

In their teaching approach, the authors also have utilized concepts advanced by case grammarians. Fillmore, who introduced the term "case grammar," suggests that the deep structure of every simple sentence consists of a verb plus a number of noun phrases that hold special cases or functional relations to the verb.[16] He says that case notions constitute a set of universal concepts that identify certain types of judgments people are capable of making about events. Perception of these events involves understandings about such matters as who did what, to whom, and what got changed. Fillmore believes these judgments are "presumably innate." Hence, case relationships seem to reflect and relate to internalized organizations of reality. From the authors' point of view, case relationships equate with semantic relationships.

Chafe provides a number of classifications of case relationships.[17] For example, in the sentence, "The wood is dry," the verb is a "state" verb because the wood is in the state of being dry. The noun "wood" is described as "patient" because it is not doing anything nor is anything being done to it. The relationship is that of state-patient. In "The dish broke," the verb is a "process" verb since the noun's state or condition has been changed. The relationship is process-patient. In the sentence "Harry ran," the relationship is action-agent because the agent (Harry) caused the action (ran).

Not all grammarians agree on the identification of such specific semantic relationships. The authors have used Chafe's classifications in this approach because they seem to be applicable to teaching. However, it must be recognized that case grammar is not a full-blown grammar and, to some extent, the term "grammar" is a misnomer.[18]

The authors believe their approach to teaching reading and writing is on strong ground for it is firmly rooted in the notion that semantic relationships and networks should be employed to bridge the gap between meaning and grammar. (Models of text, mental processes, and the interactions between text and processes in reading and writing are presented in Chapter 4 and the sequence of practical applications based on these models in Chapters 5 through 14.)

CONCLUSION

Language consists of content, form, and function. Often approaches to reading and writing have focused on form almost to the exclusion of function and content. Although function, form, and content are indivisible in normal language use, emphasis often needs to be placed, initially, on function and content for the beginning writer/reader. When form is overemphasized, pupils develop inappropriate and ineffective schemata for reading and writing. Once pupils internalize the awareness and the knowledge that the major purpose of language is to convey meaning by presenting content, they can consider form. In reading, awareness of structure can aid comprehension. In writing, putting the content into a given form is essential so that what the writer wants to convey can be interpreted by the reader. The semantic organizer approach develops function, content, and form in an appropriate sequence.

NOTES

1. Grover C. Mathewson, "The Function of Attitude in the Reading Process," in *Theoretical Models and Processes of Reading*, ed. Harry Singer and Robert Ruddell (Newark, Del.: International Reading Association, 1976).
2. John D. Bransford and Nancy S. McCarrell, "A Sketch of a Cognitive Approach to Comprehension: Some Thoughts About What It Means to Comprehend," in *Cognition and the Symbolic Processes*, ed. Walter B. Weimer and David S. Palermo (Elizabeth, N.J.: Lawrence Erlbaum Associates, 1974).
3. Anthony Van Uden, *A World of Language for the Deaf* (St. Michielsgestel, The Netherlands: The Institute for the Deaf, 1968).
4. H. Alan Robinson, *Teaching Reading and Study Strategies: the Content Areas* (Boston: Allyn and Bacon, Inc., 1978), 137.
5. Judy Rash, Terry D. Johnson, and Norman Gleadow, "Acquisition and Retention of Written Words by Kindergarten Children Under Varying Learning Conditions," *Reading Research Quarterly* 19, no. 4 (Summer 1984): 452–60.
6. Eve Clark, "What's in a Word? On the Child's Acquisition of Semantics in His First Language," in *Cognitive Development and the Acquisition of Language*, ed. Timothy E. Moore (New York: Academic Press, Inc., 1973).
7. Joseph Church, *Language and the Discovery of Reality* (New York: Random House, Inc., 1961).
8. Frank Smith, *Understanding Reading* (Holt, Rinehart & Winston, Inc., 1978), 129.

9. Noam Chomsky, *Syntactic Structures* (The Hague: Mouton Publishers, 1957).

10. Roger Brown, *A First Language* (Cambridge, Mass.: Harvard University Press, 1973).

11. Michael A.K. Halliday, *Exploration in the Functions of Language* (London: Edward Arnold, Ltd., 1973).

12. _____, *Exploration in the Development of Language* (Amsterdam: North-Holland Publishing Company, 1977).

13. Melissa Bowerman, "Structural Relations in Children's Utterances," in *Cognitive Development and the Acquisition of Language*, ed. Timothy E. Moore (New York: Academic Press, Inc., 1973).

14. Lois Bloom, *One Word at a Time* (The Hague: Mouton Publishers, 1973).

15. Halliday, *Exploration in the Functions of Language*.

16. Charles Fillmore, "The Case for Case," in *Universals in Linguistic Theory*, ed. Emmon Bach and Robert Harms (New York: Holt, Rinehart & Winston, Inc., 1968).

17. Wallace Chafe, *Meaning and the Structure of Language* (Chicago: The University of Chicago Press, 1970).

18. Terry Winograd, *Language as a Cognitive Process: Syntax* (Reading, Mass.: Addison-Wesley Publishing Company, 1983).

Chapter 4

Interactive Models

The authors' approach to the teaching of writing and reading is based on the underpinnings presented in Chapters 1, 2, and 3. This chapter synthesizes ideas presented previously and offers the authors' own models that demonstrate interactions between text and mental processes and between reading and writing.

The teacher's most important role in a reading lesson is played before the student's reading or writing. The teacher helps youngsters prepare to read through preorganizing ideas and, when necessary, increasing the proximity between author and reader. Brainstorming, questioning, and diagraming relationships are ways of helping learners mobilize their own prior experiences to bring them to the reading. Visual and auditory aids, real experiences, brainstorming, questioning, and diagraming relationships are means of increasing author–reader proximity.

The teacher's most important role in a writing lesson also is played before the writing—during the outpouring of ideas and the first organization of those ideas. Hayes and Flower point to three ingredients of the planning process in writing: generating, organizing, and goal setting.[1] The initial organizing usually consists of labeling ideas and arranging them in some way to form a coherent structure. When learners are not given the opportunity to do this and try immediately to put ideas into sentence form, they often write in disoriented fashion.

For example, at a very simple level, Jackie wants to write about her pet kitten. She should first get her ideas out in any way and in any order she can: "My kitten Gruff, black with a white tip on her tail, runs fast, purrs when happy, meows when hungry, often bad." Then, before any orderly writing takes place, she should organize the information primarily at a semantic rather than syntactic level:

PREPLAN-NING

Semantic intent, related to the Hayes and Flower notion of goal setting, is the specific meaning a speaker or writer wants to convey to a given listener or reader. In oral language, semantic intent can be assisted via nonlinguistic or extralinguistic information such as facial expressions, intonation, and body language as well as the total contextual situation shared by the speaker and listener.[2]

In written language a writer must provide cues and a reader must look for cues in the broad linguistic context. As suggested earlier, a context larger than a sentence usually is essential for understanding relationships within most sentences. The reader needs to hold actively in memory the topic of the larger context and continually needs to relate ideas represented by many individual sentences to that topic. The author or writer also is required to hold the topic in mind and to fit each sentence into successively logical paragraphs. For instance, a sentence like "Why did they do that?" is well formed but meaningless in terms of semantic intent unless the reader or the writer relates it to previous sentences that describe actions taken by agents that resulted in the event alluded to as "that."

As in that example, sentences with pronouns always need to relate to a broader context. But the same is true of most isolated sentences. For example, in such a simple sentence as "John walked to the store," the semantic intent is hazy without more context. Does the writer want to emphasize that it was John and not Mary who went to the store? Does the writer want to stress that John walked to the store rather than to the bowling alley?

Without understanding the writer's semantic intent, it may even be impossible to figure out the appropriate pronunciation of some words. For instance, in "They had a row on the lake," the word "row" could rhyme with "low" or "cow," depending upon the larger context.

Organization is the base for the successful comprehension or production of semantic intent. Semantic intent depends on relationships of parts to whole. The writer who is not clear about the semantic organization will confuse readers and fail to communicate. The reader who fails to organize ideas in ways similar to the author's will fail to comprehend the intended meaning. Semantic organizing, introduced in practical forms in the following chapters, is a prerequisite and essential to the communication of semantic intent.

TEXT

A text is an organized unit of written language, larger than a sentence, minimally a paragraph, and usually many paragraphs. A text is composed of interdependent cuing systems, referred to earlier, that provide readers with mapping systems aimed at mobilizing their ability to interpret the writers' intended meanings. The basic cuing systems are: (a) orthography (governed by rules that dictate how graphemes and morphemes may combine to form words); (b) syntactic structures (governed by rules that indicate how words are ordered sequentially within sentences); (c) semantic relationships; and (d) text organization.

Semantic relationships are governed by rules of language and logic. They demonstrate connections in meanings at sentence and intersentence levels. Semantic relationships represent the connected meanings intended by the writer.

Text organization incorporates all of the other cuing systems in order to represent information of various kinds in an overall organized way. In a superordinate-subordinate (topic plus supporting information) pattern or in a sequential presentation, organized text may make use of paragraphing, headings, key sentences, etc. Figure 4–1 illustrates how parts of a text relate to one another.

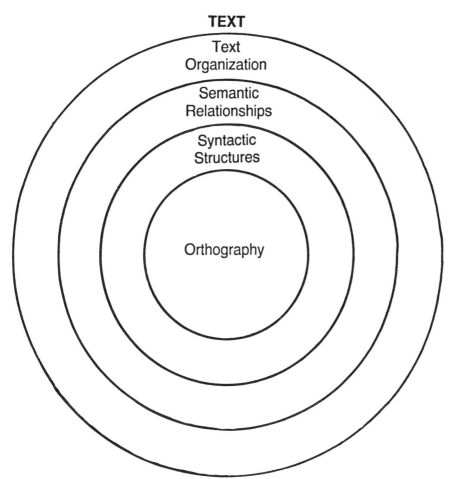

Figure 4–1
How Parts of a
Text Interrelate

PROCESSES

In reading and writing, learners process data in ways that interact with text. These processes are influenced strongly by the readers' and the writers' cultural, affective, cognitive, and linguistic domains. Cultural and affective domains energize cognitive and linguistic domains. Linguistic processes are dependent at all times on cognitive processes. Figure 4–2 represents a model of how the various processes interrelate.

The outside ring of this model, cognitive organizing (of ideas), influences all other components. Learners need, above all, to learn to organize their experiences; without organization, language processing is of no practical value.

The next ring represents semantic relating, the use of ideas organized in internal schemata but represented as language forms. In the semantic organizer approach, such organizations of ideas are represented as networks of key words.

Syntactic structuring, the third ring, frequently represents a difficult step for youngsters, as indicated earlier. In writing, when children try to remember ideas and,

Figure 4–2
How Linguistic
Processes
Interrelate

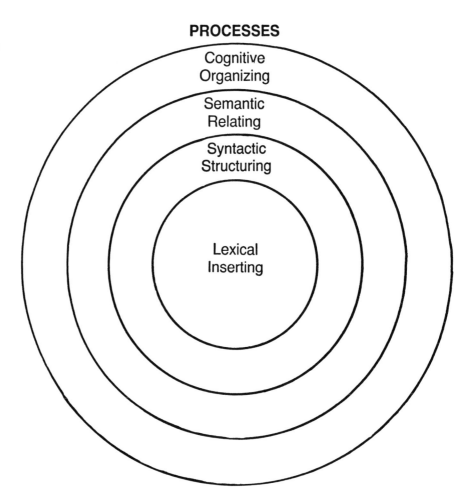

PROCESSES

Cognitive
Organizing

Semantic
Relating

Syntactic
Structuring

Lexical
Inserting

at the same time, relate them meaningfully to the construction of sentences, frustration often results. In reading, frustration also occurs when children attempt to synthesize and remember a topic and related meanings while simultaneously trying to decode the meanings of transformed and complex sentences. Too often they attempt to focus on sentence structuring before they cement semantic organizing; indeed, many teachers have had the problem of a half-written sentence with no ending in the pupil's mind. It is best to concentrate on syntax, without worrying about losing organized meanings, once the meanings are represented graphically as semantic organizers.

The last and inner ring, lexical inserting, involves using individual words in sentences. A lexicon is an internalized, dictionary-like structure consisting of an individual's own personal vocabulary. In actuality, this lexicon is utilized in part in conjunction with semantic relating; however, in writing, once the syntactic structure is formulated in the mind, the lexicon must be activated and appropriate words must be accessed to complete the sentences.

CONCLUSION

In reading and writing, processes and text parallel one another in such ways that each process interacts with the parallel aspect of the text. Cognitive organizing interacts with text organization, semantic relating with semantic relationships, syntactic structuring with syntactic structures, and lexical inserting with orthography.

Many approaches to the teaching of reading and writing (particularly as interconnected processes) have not dealt strongly enough with the interrelationships of cues in text and processes of the mind. Cognitive organizing and semantic relating have been, to some extent, missing links—or at least weak ones—in instructional situations. The results of the authors' feelings on this issue, and their work with thousands of learners, form the semantic organizer approach in subsequent chapters.

NOTES

1. John R. Hayes and Linda Flower, "Identifying the Organization of Writing Processes," in *Cognitive Processes in Writing*, ed. Lee W. Gregg and Erwin R. Steinberg (Hillsdale, N.J.: Lawrence Erlbaum Associates, 1980).
2. Francesco Antinucci and Domenico Parisi, "Early Semantic Development in Child Language," in *Foundations of Language Development: A Multidisciplinary Approach*, vol. 1, ed. Eric Lenneberg and Elizabeth Lenneberg (New York: Academic Press, Inc., 1975).

Strategies for the Semantic Organizer Approach

Chapter 5

Beginning

Six types of semantic organizers demonstrate the sequence of instruction in the following chapters. The six types are: realia and picture (Chapter 5), verb (Chapter 6), noun (Chapter 7), concept (Chapter 8), and episodic (Chapter 9). This chapter presents ideas and specific suggestions for preparing pupils to read and write, emphasizing and describing realia and picture organizers.

The optimal time for beginning instruction in reading and writing appears to depend on two factors: the approach and the attitude of the teacher. A child may be ready to learn if one type of instruction is available but unready if another approach is tried.[1] The child needs to be successful and the approach needs to make sense—to that child. The teacher must have a positive attitude about the approach and expect the pupil to be successful.

The teacher needs to recognize each child's strengths and build on them. Most children have major strengths in their abilities to organize their own worlds. A teacher may notice that children can organize their own possessions. They may demonstrate this by placing clothing (hat and coat) in a closet and books, pencils, crayons, etc., on a desk. They demonstrate organizational abilities and strengths by anticipating events at a particular time of the day. At 10 a.m. they walk toward the gymnasium rather than the lunchroom. In such ways they demonstrate both spatial and temporal organization skills. These should be noted and communicated as strengths to the children.

A strong base in oral language is desirable but not essential for initiating instruction in reading and writing, although success certainly can be achieved more quickly if the child has good ability in receptive comprehension. Children need to have sufficient comprehension skills and attention span to undertake skills basic to learning to read

ASSESSMENT OF READINESS

and to write. Those ready for such learning should be able to sequence two or three pictures, especially those directly related to their own experiences. For example, after a trip to a zoo a child should be able to pick three photos and place them in a sequential order (not necessarily left to right) and demonstrate what happened first, second, and third during the experience (e.g., traveling to the zoo, at the zoo, coming home).

The way children play is a good indicator of their readiness for reading and writing. For example, a child who places a cup in water and pretends it is a boat and the child who dresses with a cape and pretends to fly are demonstrating understanding and appreciation basic to dealing with imaginative stories.

Very young children who enjoy drawing pictures and telling stories about them show an inclination toward representing their experiences on paper and sharing them with others. As they arrange pictures in sequence, they demonstrate real ability to organize and compose. Readiness for writing becomes more apparent as children scribble and "read back" stories. Teachers can note the growing maturity in readiness for writing by observing the development of differentiation of the marks that are being scribbled and by the repetition of certain marks when words they speak are repeated. As children consistently use certain kinds of scribbling to represent certain words, they are moving rapidly toward actual composing that can be read by others. Usually these children begin to introduce letters into their scribbling.

Children who feel they are communicating by writing make a clear distinction between drawing and writing. For example, if such a child is asked to draw a picture first and then asked to write a secret message that no one else needs to understand, the message usually will be horizontal as distinguished from the varied directionalities of the picture. The message may resemble writing dependent upon the child's knowledge of letters.

Similarly, children who are developing a readiness for reading have been pretending to be reading over a period of time. They are often the children who also are reading stories based on their own "writing." Children who want to read will interpret pictures and tell a story through the pictures. They will remember much of a story after hearing it and will pretend to read the story as they leaf through a book. They quickly begin to recognize certain words that are repeated often, or that are unusual in shape, or that stand for meaningful things in the child's life—like McDonald's, their own names, street signs, etc.

Observations of such behaviors, and respectful interactions with young children about what they are doing, are probably more accurate assessments of readiness in reading and writing than any type of formal testing. In fact, skills tested in formal readiness tests may have little to do with functional reading and writing abilities. Many children fail to demonstrate their potential and strengths through such measures. Readiness tests frequently contain auditory and visual discrimination tasks involving geometric shapes or pictures unrelated to writing and reading schemata[2] and fail to demonstrate children's strengths. Rather than contrived artificial situations for assessments, observations of the child in natural classroom situations seem more valid for estimating readiness for instruction in reading and writing and the presence or absence of a writing or reading schema. Certainly the child who plays at reading and writing is demonstrating the existence of such schemata.

Probably the most accurate and practical way to assess readiness for specific activities is to observe the results of teaching. If the child learns, then readiness is apparent; however, if the child fails to learn, certain questions should be considered:

- Did the teacher provide a purpose for the activity?
- Did the child understand the purpose?
- Did the child have prior prerequisite experience?
- If not, did the teacher provide the necessary experience?
- Was instruction related to the child's schema?
- Was instruction based on a natural expansion of the child's strengths?
- Did the teacher expect the child to succeed?
- Did the child expect to succeed?

The child is most likely to demonstrate readiness if the approach, the teacher, and the experiential base are considered and dealt with appropriately. The degree of match between the learner and the instructional tasks that optimize the chances for success must be the major consideration in assessing readiness.

TEACHER ATTITUDE

Probably the single most important factor in assisting a child to prepare for reading and writing is the teacher's attitude. Many times teachers need to recognize the negative effects of prior failure that may be a part of the child's history. Too often children are not ready because they have failed so often. They are afraid to try and fail again. The children or the parents or previous teachers—any or all of them—may be blamed for lack of previous development. But laying blame is not the point and is of no value. Teaching is of value. Teachers need to accept all children exactly as they are and build upon their strengths. Children need to feel the safety of the environment created by a teacher who thinks and feels positively.

To a large degree, the success or failure of learning depends on the teacher's ability not only to observe external behaviors of the children but also, in a sense, to peer into their minds. Truly great teachers seem to be able to look at the world through a child, from the child's own point of view. The sequence of activities presented here is a general instrument that needs to be tuned specifically to each child. It is essential to try to observe the meaningfulness of these activities through each child's individual point of view.

A CHILD'S POINT OF VIEW

Piaget emphasizes the importance of looking at the world of the child from the child's point of view. Too often, approaches are based on adult views. For example, it is almost axiomatic to begin with the concrete and move to the abstract. However, what adults view as "concrete" may be very different from what children might consider concrete. Adults might consider a chair or a table to be concrete things but children might not. In fact, an object may not even exist for a child until it has been acted upon.

An object itself usually will have little importance or "concreteness" even then. It is the function, the use, the action involved with the object that will be more important, more "concrete" to the child. Movement itself will gain the attention of a child before any static object will. The most important motion, of course, is the child's own action. The point is that action, not object, is the "concrete" or least abstract element to the child.

Traditional approaches to written language development usually develop nouns or adjectives (color words) first. In many classrooms, cardboard labels are taped to the furniture. It is the authors' experience that these labels soon fade from sight, both figuratively and literally. Basically, children ignore them, whether they stay taped to the furniture or are trod upon when they have fallen to the floor. Color words often are stressed but to children these seem to be even more abstract than nouns. These colors are easy to illustrate in a nonlinguistic context and thus tend to be overemphasized. However, color words rarely are found in the presyntactic or first syntactic lexicons and do not have much value for communication. This emphasis on color words has been criticized by Bloom and Lahey as early and inappropriate.[3]

As noted earlier, numerous teaching concepts seem based on the adult's view of the world rather than the child's. For example, some contend that the child's first word is a noun, so nouns should be the first words taught in reading and writing. This is worth examining first from the adult point of view. A baby seated in a highchair points to a bottle and says, "ba ba." From the adult point of view, the word "ba ba" represents bottle and would be a noun. This point of view appears to be based solely on the surface structure of the utterance, but it is necessary to examine the infant's intent in context. This further examination suggests that a parent would be most likely to get the bottle and hand it to the child. The child would grab the bottle and drink. Certainly, the child's intention would be recognized as requesting the bottle for the purpose of feeding. The baby was using the word "ba ba" not for the purpose of representing a noun but to express a functional need.

Another example: A 2-year-old girl seated on a couch suddenly shows some frustration in her activity and says, "foot." An adult seated next to her sees that the girl's foot is caught in the side of the couch. The adult helps the child release her foot. Children use nouns not in an adult way but as signals for activity. Action events are the "single most important category in children's language."[4]

Actions normally are represented in language by verbs. Young children crave activity. It is a central means for them to satiate their curiosity and to learn about the world. The very heart of a schema is action. All schemata initially develop through acting on something in the environment. For these reasons, but not for these reasons alone, actions are suggested as a beginning point for introducing language-related activities to children. Realia organizers help children relate an activity, represented by a picture (such as eating dinner, playing ball, cleaning house, fixing a car, etc.), to real objects (such as specific tools) that could be used within the context of that topic. The emphasis is on activity right from the introduction of basic readiness activities.

BASIC READINESS ACTIVITIES

A basic instructional experience is storytelling and story reading. Children who have been read to at home come to school frequently with such strong schemata related to reading and writing that they already know what is involved in these processes. Some learn how to read simply by having been read to. Here the teacher's attitude is especially important. Children who have never developed schemata related to reading and writing probably are those who have not been read to. Children who lack a sense of a story schema (for example, understanding that a story has a beginning, middle, and end) need experiences with stories.

A great teacher is a great actor or actress and can make stories come to life. When reading or telling a story, the teacher's enthusiasm for the story must leap out and catch the audience. Especially for children who have failed and have negative feelings about books, it is essential that teachers reverse this view and model their own love for books.

It also is essential that a teacher model the use of books for acquiring information. For example, when questions arise in the classroom, the teacher should be ready to turn to books for answers. It is helpful when the teacher does not know all the answers. On one occasion a group of children wanted to know whether elephants could swim. The teacher did not know but found the answer in an encyclopedia (elephants do swim).

It also is important to teach children how to play symbolically through modeling. A teacher who is going to read a story that involves children riding on a bus can line up chairs in the classroom and role-play a bus scene. Indeed, the actual experience of taking a bus trip may be a prerequisite to role playing. In such a case the teacher can take a camera along and later ask the children to put some of the pictures (two or three) in sequence, demonstrating the beginning, middle, and end of the trip.

Young children should be encouraged to play at writing as they imitate the activities of adults. Children often enjoy "reading" the stories they have "written," although the adult may not be able to decipher them. It also is interesting to note that each time the youngster "reads" the story, it may change. This play with writing and reading is an important readiness activity. It must be accepted by the teacher and by the parents of young children.

Another readiness activity that helps connect visual stimuli with imagination and language involves the use of balloon books. Children, at a very early age, can appreciate their own balloon book when it is composed of pictures directly related to real or fantasy experiences. The parent or teacher and child take and select photos. These photos can be related to actual experiences or to fantasies. They may involve a series of pictures representing a short sequence, either real or fantasy. The child should be encouraged to comment on the experiences and the parent or teacher may help draw the picture and write in a balloon form an exact dictation of the youngster's spontaneous words (see Figure 5–1).

Balloon books are helpful for encouraging reading and writing readiness activities because children soon realize that their language can be written down, saved, and is valuable. As they mature, journals and scrapbooks should be encouraged and the youngsters' language and imagination should form the core of these books. Such books are good introductions to the writing of personal experiences and feelings.

As part of this readiness activity, actual experiences and projects can be preserved in photo books. For example, one youngster who lived in New York City developed a scale model of the Brooklyn Bridge. He took photos of it and produced a small picture book with written captions that he was able to read.

Figure 5–1
Balloon
Captures the
Child's Own
Words

Activities involving the sequencing of activities and real experiences, as well as storytelling and reading, are important readiness activities and bases for the future development of episodic organizers. However, long before the introduction of such organizers (Chapter 9), children need to learn to categorize actions and things in relation to a given topic—categorization of subordinate comments or subtopics under a superordinate (major topic or idea).

REALIA ORGANIZERS

This process begins with realia organizers. Such organizers are useful in the nursery school and kindergarten or at other levels where such action organizing seems necessary. A child constructs a realia organizer by using a large picture, pieces of rope, and real objects to demonstrate relationships involving a topic and related activities. The topic must involve activity; the real objects must be related to the activity; the child must be involved in the activity through the construction of the organizer. Activity is central.

Teachers should provide pictures that represent activities related to the child's experiences. For example, they can find four real things that would be used in relation to the activity represented in a picture and also choose one real thing unrelated to the picture. (See Figure 5–2.) The teacher cuts five pieces of rope about two feet long and a sixth a foot long, then demonstrates the activity. The core is a large picture of a group of people eating at a dinner table. Holding a plate, the teacher asks the children if it belongs with the picture. If all agree, the plate is placed on a table near the large picture. Next, a two-foot piece of rope is used to connect the picture and the plate.

Figure 5–2
A Realia
Organizer

The teacher shows other items such as a cup, glass, and knife and, when children agree that these are related, connects them individually to the picture with a two-foot piece of rope for each (inclusive categories). Now the teacher picks up an item that would not appear to be related to the dinner scene, such as a toy car, and asks if it belongs with the picture. If children agree that the car does not belong, it is placed near the picture and also connected to it with a two-foot piece of rope. The one-foot piece of rope then is placed at right angles across and about in the middle of the connecting rope. The children are told that this rope means "no," the car does not belong (exclusive category). Of course, if a child has a reason for disagreeing with the majority opinion, that point of view should be considered important.

After the realia organizer is completed and all children seem to understand why and how it was constructed, the teacher removes all the real objects and asks the children to reconstruct it. They may place items in different corners but the inclusive and exclusive categories should be indicated appropriately by the pieces of rope. If they have no problems in constructing the same organizer, the teacher takes another picture of an active scene, such as a mechanic repairing an automobile. (Whatever scene is chosen, the children must have had experiences related to that activity.) The teacher provides five items—four tools and an unrelated object such as the plate used in the previous organizer—then asks the pupils to make their own organizer using this new picture and the real items.

Children should practice with varied realia organizers until each can manage several of them independently. Independence is important if children are to internalize this organizational pattern as a base for what is to follow. Through this type of activity, they really begin to understand superordinate/subordinate and inclusive/exclusive relationships.

PICTURE ORGANIZERS

Picture organizers frequently give youngsters their first real notion that things can be symbolized through pictures and are not the things themselves. They also get an opportunity to use picture symbols in organizing relationships.

Teachers should acquire from magazines, newspapers, old workbooks, etc., fairly large pictures that represent a single action; they also can take photographs of children performing specific actions such as jumping, running, or swimming. Large, simple, stick-figure sketches of such specific actions also could be used.

Because these pictures also form the base for much of the initial work with semantic organizers, it is vital that children understand the activity represented. The teacher asks them to demonstrate what is happening in the picture, perhaps by pantomiming the activity. The way the question is phrased is important. The intent should be, "What is happening?" not "What do you see?" Pupils must understand that they are to describe action, not just objects or people in the picture.

This should be repeated with as many pictures as the teacher can find. The teacher particularly should look for, take, or draw pictures of running, swimming, jumping, flying, walking, laughing, eating, drinking. A series of smaller pictures of objects from magazines and newspapers will enable the children to develop picture organizers the same way they did for realia organizers. For example, to start, the teacher can use the picture of people eating at a table that was included in the original realia organizer, using pictures to replace the objects: knife, plate, glass, cup, car. After the teacher models that organizer, the children do similar ones.

Lollypop Stick Figures

Some youngsters are helped best by using something like the authors' stick figure, Lollypop. The teacher shows a picture of Lollypop doing an activity and asks the pupils to imitate it. With some children, the teacher may have to perform the activity first, then have them imitate it. Eventually all pupils should be able to imitate the activity just by seeing Lollypop.

Once children can respond automatically to a picture of Lollypop involved in an activity, they can be encouraged to name the action. For example, the teacher informs the children, who are seated, that they are going to play a game with Lollypop, then shows a picture of Lollypop sitting down (Figure 5–3). The teacher indicates that Lollypop is doing the same thing they are doing—sitting in chairs.

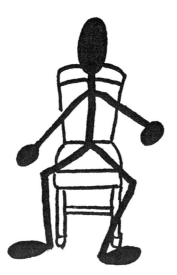

Figure 5–3
Lollypop

The pupils are told next that Lollypop will be doing something else in the picture and they will be asked to do the same thing. The teacher shows a picture of Lollypop standing, which the youngsters should imitate; then a picture of Lollypop sitting is shown, which the children again should imitate. In cementing the symbolization process and the knowledge of verb actions, many other pictures of Lollypop can be shown—drinking, walking, swimming, etc. (See Figure 5–4.)

After children can perform a few actions, they should be called upon to identify the action through language. Since action schemata are all prerequisites for language, children should perform the action before producing language. Action links language to thought. The pupils should learn to use the imperative verb form in their oral language—sit, stand, drink, etc. This will prepare them for the next step of using words (imperative verbs) with pictures.

Verbs of action, particularly in initial reading and writing, are extremely important for interpreting sentence meanings. The learning of nouns and adjectives as first words does not lead naturally to an understanding of how words interact to represent

Picture Organizers with Verbs

Figure 5–4
Lollypop the Activist in Motion

cognitive relationships or to an understanding of sentence meanings. Verbs are different. Many can stand alone and represent an entire grammatical form.

The teacher introduces a written verb by showing the picture of Lollypop. (See Figure 5–5.) The children perform the actions. The teacher then says, "Lollypop is telling you what to do. What is Lollypop saying? Show me." (Cued by the picture, most youngsters have little trouble with the question.) The teacher then tells the pupils to perform the action first, then say the word. Balloon figures are practiced with all verbs previously learned: Children first perform the action, then say the word. (Deaf children may "sign" the verbs.)

The teacher then makes up pictures with empty balloons and shows the children how to insert an appropriate verb.

The pupils next can play a "concentration" game, starting with pictures and words turned face down. About five verbs and five matching pictures are used for review. Each child takes a turn and turns over two cards, a picture of Lollypop and a verb. If the Lollypop action picture matches the verb, the child keeps those cards. If they do not match, the child replaces them face down. The winner is the child with the most cards at the end.

More verbs are introduced by using Lollypop alone, then with the balloons, and finally by matching verbs and pictures.

Generalizing Actions

The pictures involved in the previous exercises can be used, with additional ones as appropriate. All pictures should be of animals or people performing actions such as running, jumping, etc. For example, the teacher provides four pictures of running—dogs, cats, children, and horses—and one of an object that cannot run, such as a table, chair, or lamp. The pictures are placed on a large piece of colored background paper (green or dark blue), with another smaller piece of paper (red or orange) adjoining the first. The children are asked if all the pictures belong on the green paper. They need to find the one picture (such as the table) that does not belong. The teacher removes that picture and puts it on the smaller red paper. All the pictures then are returned to the green paper and a child is asked to take the one that does not belong and put it on the red paper.

The next exercise uses a different set of pictures, such as frogs, boys, fish, and girls jumping, plus a table. The pupils should be able to choose the picture that does not belong.

Next, a written verb is included in the set. This can be Lollypop performing and "saying" the action. Children should be able to identify the major category and put the verb in the center of the green paper.

Another reinforcer for the generalizing and categorization process involves using pictures of actions and two verbs. This requires two large pieces of paper of different colors (e.g., one green, one blue) and two different sets of pictures. Only pictures that can be categorized into one of two classes of actions should be used.

For example, the teacher can provide four pictures of animals or people running, four pictures of animals or people jumping, and the two verbs—run and jump—written on cards. The teacher demonstrates by putting the verb card "run" on one paper (the green paper, for example), then the verb card "jump" on the blue paper.

Figure 5–5
Lollypop Learns
to Talk

All the pictures representing "jump" are placed on the blue paper and the pictures representing "run" are placed on the green paper. The pupils then repeat the activity. All verbs and action pictures are reviewed using the same method.

ACTION-AGENT RELATION-SHIPS

An action-agent relationship involves some person or animate creature performing an action. Since many youngsters know how to read their names before coming to school, the teacher can introduce this type of activity by using cards bearing the children's names along with the written form of the verb. (Children should be encouraged to write their names on their papers for identification purposes. Their names also should appear on their possessions and in places where they keep them.)

In combining names and actions the teacher holds up a verb card and the pupils all perform the action. The teacher then holds up a child's name card, then a verb card. When the cards together say, for example, "John run," then John should run (or cards that say, "John sit"). Simple Simon type games can be played in this way. The nouns "Boys" and "Girls" (with initial capital letters) also can be introduced. (Nouns are introduced with capital letters because they will be the initial words in sentences the children will soon write and read.) Most pupils can be successful with this activity because initially a boy may need to know and watch only for his own name; later, he would have to be alert to respond to the verb when the noun "Boys" is presented.

Another activity that extends action-agent relationships involves having children dress in symbolic costumes. For example, one pupil may have dog ears made from cardboard tied around the head, another with rabbit ears, another with cardboard wings on the back, another with an elephant's trunk, and another with fins like a fish. The teacher then holds up a verb such as "swim" and the children "swim" the way the animal they represent would swim. The child with the fins would swim like a fish, the one with dog ears would dog paddle. Some would not swim at all while others might need to learn whether or not animals they represent can swim.

By developing understandings of action-agent relationships in these ways, teachers can capitalize on children's strengths and make learning fun and easy.

CONCLUSION

All children have strengths upon which to build. Most strengths lie in their ability to organize their experiences. By building reading and writing schemata upon these strengths, children who may fail with other approaches can be successful with the one presented here. Youngsters who have failed with other methods may need success fast. The approach to beginning reading and writing presented in this chapter offers a sequential development of activities that is successful for most pupils, although the teacher may need to adapt them for specific situations.

A major advantage of these beginning activities is that the child is active throughout and can see and feel progress through involvement. It is essential that the teacher challenge each child appropriately so that both challenges and successes are real.

A child who has been involved in the activities suggested here will be able to categorize pictures of actions, respond to action verbs, respond to action-agent relationships, and construct an organizer using real objects and pictures. These activities lead directly into the development of verb organizers discussed in the next chapter.

1. Dolores Durkin, "What Does Research Say About the Time to Begin Reading Instruction?" *Journal of Educational Research* 64, no. 2 (1970): 53–56.

2. Joanne R. Nurss, "Research in the Assessment of Prereading Skills—An American Perspective," *Reading* 13, no. 1 (April 1979): 21–29.

3. Lois Bloom and Margaret Lahey, *Language Development and Language Disorders* (New York: John Wiley & Sons, Inc., 1978).

4. Ibid.

NOTES

Chapter 6

Verb Organizers

This chapter explains, develops, and demonstrates verb organizers. A sequence of steps is suggested. This sequence is based on practical experiences in working with children; however, it is not the one and only sequence. Because children differ, the sequence may have to be adapted to their individual needs. The rate and amount of practice at each step also may vary, depending on the learner. A youngster with a severe language learning problem will move through the steps slowly. If a child learns rapidly, the teacher should never prolong the steps but should move on as rapidly as the youngster can.

A verb organizer is a semantic organizer built on a child's understanding of several action verbs. Verb organizers teach students basic semantic relationships, first among verbs and pictures, then among verbs and nouns. Verb organizers teach the basic organization of a paragraph without emphasizing construction of syntax (word order in fully formed sentences).

ROLE OF THE VERB ORGANIZER

Very young children can learn how to construct and to comprehend relationships in verb organizers. These are natural expansions of relationships in readiness activities. They capitalize on the pupils' interest in, and need for, action. Relationships of action verbs and of agents who perform the actions are emphasized initially. Verb organizers, as do all subsequent semantic organizers, emphasize the important role of semantically related words within larger contexts. Verb organizers prepare students for understanding relationships in written language. They form the initial base for organizing ideas related to writing and reading paragraphs.

Verb organizers, as with all of the authors' organizers, are presented effectively through modeling. This means that the teacher first constructs the verb organizer, then the child produces the same organizer. The teacher next alters the organizer slightly to make sure the pupil understands the principles.

Verb organizers' development always is based on what the child already knows, introducing new relationships slowly in each subsequent organizer. Practice is essential. Children can be asked to develop an organizer a few times a day for short periods. This is particularly important for youngsters who have short attention spans. Pupils usually find organizers interesting but, like anything else, too much pressure at one time can cause that interest to flag. Short lessons are more effective than long-drawn-out ones. Examples of short sessions involving verb organizers, along with teaching ideas, are presented in this chapter.

PREPARA-TION

The teacher first collects small pictures of inanimate objects and animate beings such as animals. These pictures should measure about one or two inches square. Action verbs (previously taught) should be printed on 5″ × 8″ index cards.

Since this is a cognitively based approach, the learners should have had experiences with all the inanimate objects, animals, and people represented in the pictures. Before introducing any picture, the teacher should check to make certain the pupils have had related experience. If they have not, it will be necessary either to use another picture or to build an experience through activities, films, pictures, etc.

VERB ORGANIZERS WITH PICTURES

Before developing this step further, the teacher must make sure the children can respond appropriately to at least five action verbs. It also is helpful if they can say the verb—deaf children can sign. (Activities in Chapter 5 may be reviewed if there is a need.)

The teacher collects pictures of animals and people involved in an activity, prepares six or seven pieces of heavy string cut into one-foot lengths, and provides a large piece of colored paper on a clear desk top.

For a quick review, and as a preassessment, the teacher shows the children one of the action verbs and instructs them to act out what it says. After they have done so, the verb (in lower-case letters) is placed in the center of the paper. For example, the teacher chooses the verb "fly," then picks up a picture of butterflies and asks: "Do butterflies fly?" (Each picture should contain at least two animals, people, or inanimate objects so that the plural form of the noun will match the pictures.) After the children have agreed, the teacher places the picture on one corner of the large paper and joins that picture to the verb with one piece of string. The same is done with two other pictures, such as "bees" and "birds." The teacher then picks up a picture of two inanimate objects, such as two tables, and asks: "Do tables fly?" When the children have agreed that tables do not fly, the picture of the tables is placed on another corner of the large paper. That picture is joined to the verb with the string. To indicate that tables do not fly, the teacher places a second string diagonally across the middle of the first string.

This activity is repeated, using pictures, verbs, and strings with as many verbs as children have learned. After they have demonstrated success, they will be ready for the construction of verb organizers by using paper and pencils (or crayons).

Verbs taught in a spelling program should be included; then gradually, the spelling of the nouns introduced later in this chapter is taught. After children can respond and identify verbs and nouns, these can be used to form the core of the spelling program.

In this next step, it is important to be sure again that the children know the meaning of the verb that will be central to the organizer. In the verb organizer in Figure 6–1, the children need to know the written form of the verb "fly." (Children demonstrate the action first.) The verb card is placed in the center of a large piece of paper. (A speck of rubber cement or glue on the back will help hold it in place.) The teacher holds up a picture of birds and asks if they fly. The picture is placed on one of the corners with glue on the back and a single line is drawn from the verb to the picture.

Holding the picture of butterflies, the teacher asks if they fly, then places this picture in another corner and draws a single line. The same is done with the bees, then with the chairs, again placing each picture in a corner and drawing a line to the verb. However, when the children agree that chairs do not fly, the teacher draws another line diagonally across the first one and tells the pupils that that will be known as the "don't" line.

After the teacher has finished constructing the verb organizer, each child is asked to do the same. It is best if materials are prepared in advance so each pupil can produce a verb organizer. Another example is shown in Figure 6–2.

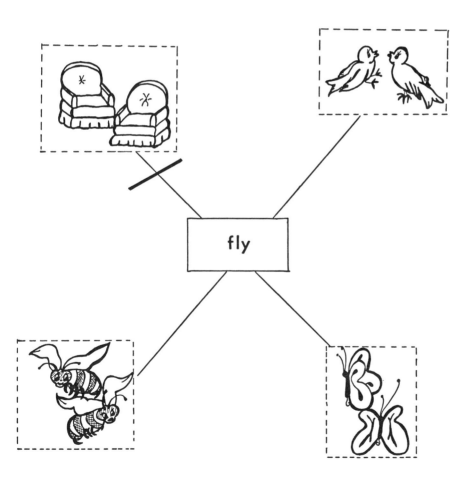

Figure 6–1
How to
Construct a
Verb Organizer

Figure 6–2
Verb Organizer

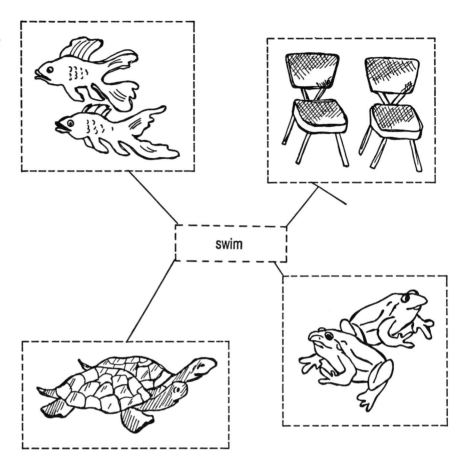

The "don't" line is not always in the same location on the paper. The children should not think that the location on the page specifies the exclusive category (the object or animal that does not represent the action). The "don't" line indicates this exclusion.

Children should be given a great deal of practice. All the verbs they initially learned should be used in such organizers. Then new verbs should be added; however, they should be introduced through readiness activities, as suggested in the previous chapter.

Youngsters will be learning very basic notions about language and organization of thoughts through this practice. They should be developing understandings that individual words do not convey all the information by themselves but that words in combination with other words (especially nouns and verbs) provide specific information. They also will be introduced to the basic organization of a paragraph with four potential sentences. They will begin to learn there is a topic and there are comments related to that topic in a paragraph organization.

After the children have become familiar with basic verb organizers and can demonstrate an understanding of at least 10 action verbs, they should be introduced to the printed forms of nouns. The teacher prints the appropriate plural nouns with the first letter of each word in capital (upper-case) letters. This will help the transition to paragraph writing later. Plural nouns are preferable because the verb then remains a consistent form. The written forms of these nouns should be printed or pasted just below the picture of the two animals or people and on the same piece of paper. Figure 6–3 is a verb organizer with printed nouns as well as pictures.

VERB ORGANIZER WITH PICTURES AND WORDS

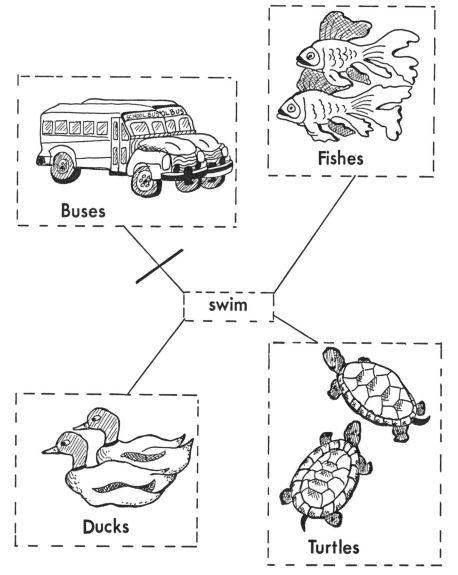

Figure 6–3
Verb Organizers
Acquire Nouns

All the verb organizers already learned can be reconstructed but with the emphasis now on the nouns. In introducing nouns, the teaching of the words in isolation should be avoided. Children should not simply match pictures and nouns; they should always work within the framework of the verb organizer, then paste the nouns below. The noun-verb relationship should be stressed. This relationship might be overlooked if the noun and pictures are simply matched on a one-to-one basis unrelated to the verb organizer.

"DON'T"

In the next set of verb organizers, the children should be introduced to the word "don't" as an indicator of the exclusive category. The word "don't" can be written on a small card and each pupil can place it on the line. The verb organizer in Figure 6–4 demonstrates where the "don't" card should be placed. Some earlier verb organizers can be reviewed with emphasis on the word "don't."

WRITING

At this point, the children should be encouraged to write the words themselves. This can be accomplished by their copying the words from an original verb organizer. These words also can be used for teaching spelling. The pupils should learn to write, or at least copy, all the verbs and nouns as well as the word "don't." (The teacher should not be concerned if, at this point, they omit the apostrophe.) For youngsters who are simply not ready or not able to write, the teacher may continue to provide printed words for assembling verb organizers.

From Organizer to Paragraph

Once the child has learned to write the words in the verb organizer, the teacher can introduce the paragraph. The pupil first constructs a verb organizer (with plural nouns) as usual. The teacher models by writing the paragraph and the children then produce the paragraph. For those who cannot write, word cards are used to construct paragraphs. Figure 6–5 demonstrates both the verb organizer and the completed paragraph.

Some syntactic principles can be developed based on verb organizers. Word order and sentence boundaries are basic principles that a child can begin to internalize. However, these principles are based on understanding relationships first at a semantic level as represented in the verb organizer.

The teacher should emphasize that the boundaries of sentences are not the end of the line on a page but the periods and capitals. These paragraphs usually contain four sentences, with the negative in the final sentence. This negative sentence contains the exclusive category and should follow logically after the inclusive, positive sentences. The pupils should produce paragraphs for all the verb organizers originally learned. They may need a great deal of practice with this, and it should be provided.

From Paragraph to Organizer

Reversibility is an important aspect of learning. Students can demonstrate that they understand how verb organizers and paragraphs are related by constructing a verb organizer after reading a paragraph. This is the reverse of the previous step. The

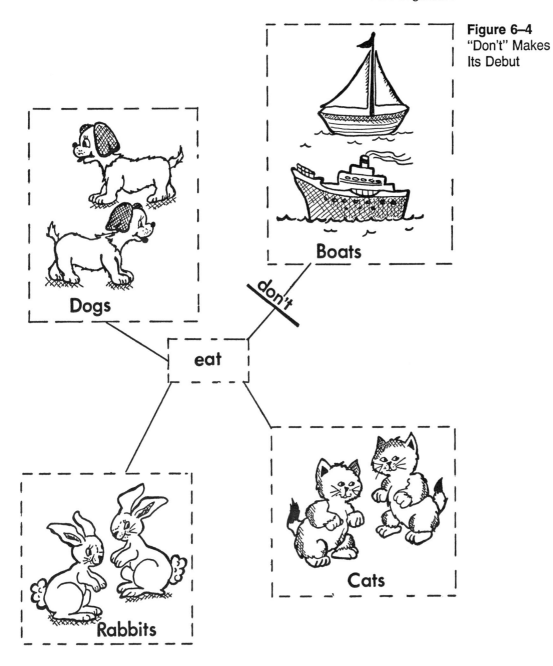

Figure 6–4
"Don't" Makes
Its Debut

paragraph is presented to the students and the teacher again models by showing how to produce the verb organizer based on the paragraph. In this verb organizer, all materials (pictures and words) are prepared for and presented to the student, who then need only assemble the organizer.

Figure 6–5
The Advent of
the Paragraph

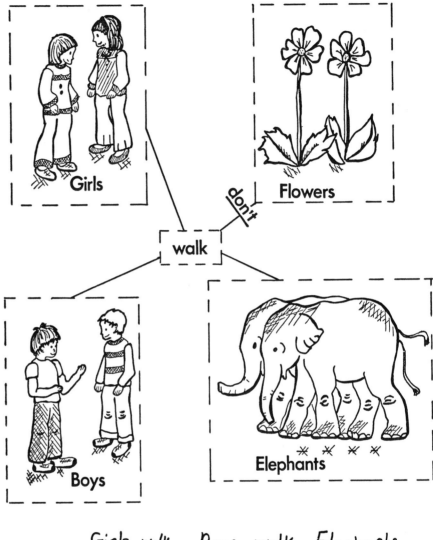

Girls walk. Boys walk. Elephants walk. Flowers don't walk.

At first, the teacher provides pictures and nouns written on the same paper. Next, the nouns are separated from the pictures so that the pupils demonstrate word knowledge within context. They then learn the written form of the nouns by writing or matching them to the picture, but not as an activity isolated from the organizer. It is important that the children learn how words function in contexts, and particularly how nouns function with verbs. The teacher should not emphasize simply matching pictures and nouns at this point. That may be developed as a review only after the pupils have demonstrated an understanding of how these words function in both organizers and paragraphs.

The learners are then expected to develop a verb organizer by writing or placing the verb in the center, pictures around the verb, and nouns under the pictures, and by drawing the appropriate lines indicating inclusive and exclusive categories. Figure 6–6 is an example of a semantic organizer based on a paragraph.

A later development of this type of activity involves the youngsters' producing the verb organizer based on the paragraph by writing the nouns under the pictures, the verb in the box, and ''don't'' on the line. In this case the teacher provides paragraphs, pictures, pencils, paper, and perhaps glue. As usual, the teacher models the construc-

Rabbits eat . Fishes
eat . Birds eat . Shoes
don't eat .

Figure 6–6
The Emergence of the Paragraph

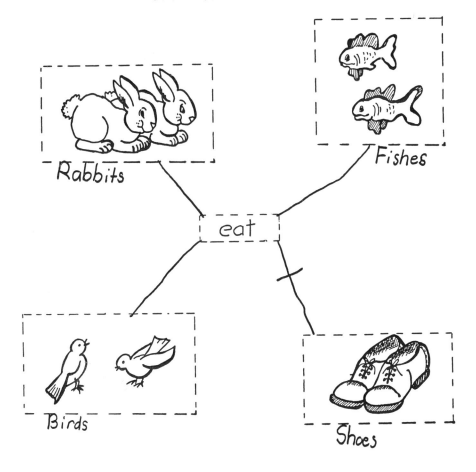

Figure 6–7
A Pupil's Own
Verb Organizer

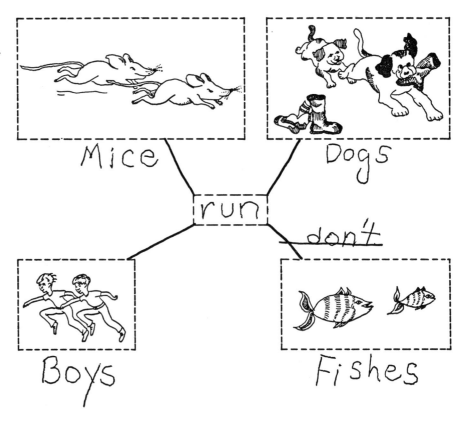

tion of the organizer before the children construct their own. Pupils should construct many organizers in the way suggested here. Some might do well to reconstruct all the organizers they have done previously. Figure 6–7 is an example of one pupil's organizer.

From Paragraph to Organizer to Paragraph

This activity eventually enables students to summarize after reading a passage. First, the paragraph is presented to the pupils, who then develop a verb organizer based on the paragraph. The original paragraph is removed (or covered) and the youngsters write a paragraph based on the semantic organizer. This paragraph does not need to be exactly the same as the original. Sentence order may differ but the relationships should remain the same. As before, the negative sentence (the "don't") usually should come last in the paragraph. Figure 6–8 is an example of another child's organizer.

Expanding

Up to this point, the verb organizers have involved three inclusive categories and one exlusive one. At this point, more categories can be added to both types—for example, four inclusive and two exclusive. The students develop this expanded organizer, then, as a separate activity, write a paragraph with appropriate positive and

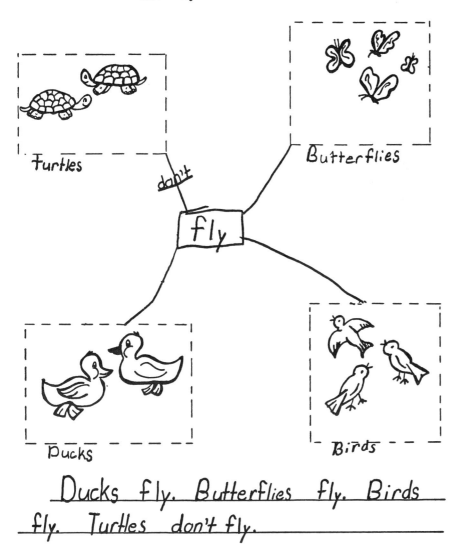

Butterflies fly . Birds fly . Ducks fly . Turtles don't fly .

Figure 6–8
Triple Play: Paragraph to Organizer to Paragraph

Turtles

don't

Butterflies

fly

Ducks

Birds

Ducks fly. Butterflies fly. Birds fly. Turtles don't fly.

negative sentences based on the expanded verb organizer. An example of an expanded verb organizer is shown in Figure 6–9.

Learners can be guided to produce "original" paragraphs based on a prepared organizer. The teacher prepares a paper by assembling about eight pictures surround-

**Writing
Independently**

Figure 6–9
The Horizon Is
Expanded

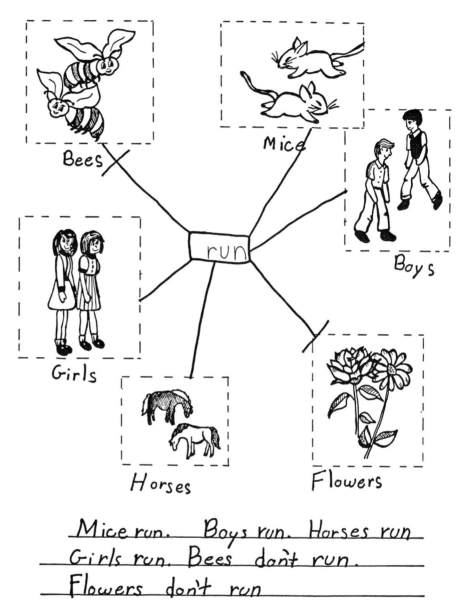

Mice run. Boys run. Horses run
Girls run. Bees don't run.
Flowers don't run

ing a verb box, then places three verb cards at the top. A pupil chooses one of the verbs, writes it in the verb box, then draws inclusive and exclusive lines from the verb to some (not necessarily all) of the pictures.

By this time, the pupils might be able to spell and write the nouns (in plural forms) under the pictures. They then write "original" paragraphs based on the verb organizer. Each pupil should be able to produce an organizer and paragraph that differs from the work of others. (See Figure 6–10.)

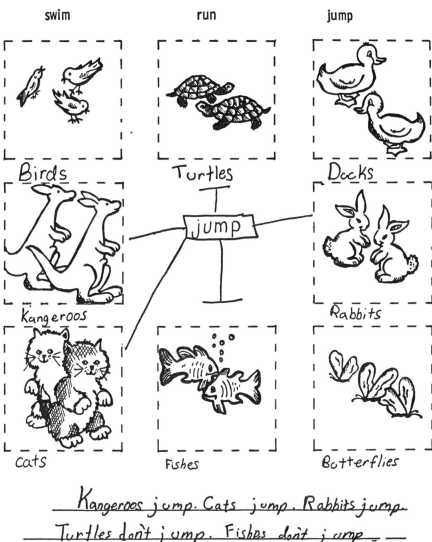

swim   run   jump

Birds   Turtles   Ducks

Kangeroos   jump   Rabbits

Cats   Fishes   Butterflies

Kangeroos jump. Cats jump. Rabbits jump.
Turtles don't jump. Fishes don't jump _____

Figure 6–10
First Steps
toward
Paragraphing

Previous verb organizers all involved verbs of action that do not take a direct object. Now the children are introduced to verb phrases. The activity of a verb becomes more specific and more meaningful when combined with a direct object in a verb phrase. The verb and direct object can be taught as a phrase as if they were one word. Figure 6–11 demonstrates such a verb organizer with a paragraph.

Instruction begins in the same manner as in the readiness part of this approach. Learners respond to verb phrases by performing the action. These new words and phrases can be added to the spelling lists. The youngsters also should have experiences with these verbs through pictures, film strips, films, etc. These verbs always should involve some action initiated by the subject (action-agent relationships).

**VERB
PHRASES**

**With Direct
Objects**

Figure 6–11
The Verbs
Discover Direct
Objects

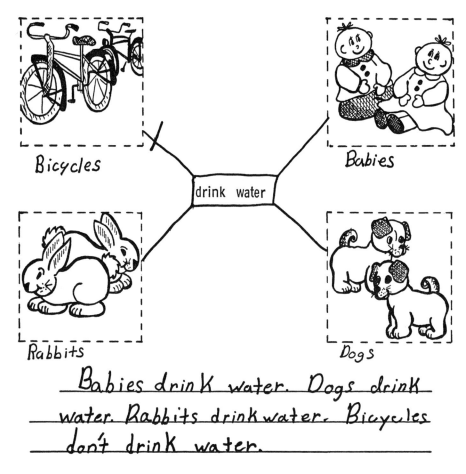

Babies drink water. Dogs drink water. Rabbits drink water. Bicycles don't drink water.

Examples of verbs with direct objects follow; however, the best lists should be based on the needs and interests of the pupils.

> eat ice cream
> draw pictures
> drink water
> wash dishes
> ride bicycles

This may be a giant step for some children with severe language needs, so much practice may be necessary. It may be important to have real objects available, such as dishes, pictures, and even ice cream, so the youngsters may learn the relationship between the action and the object.

With Indirect Objects

The indirect objects in these verb organizers are known as locatives—they designate location in relation to an action. Such verb phrases are useful in describing events in stories when the past tense of the verb is used. However, teachers should continue to use present tense verbs at this point.

Examples of verb phrases, including locatives, that might be taught at this point follow:

work in stores
fly in a plane
walk to school
ride in a truck
sleep in a bed
go to school

As in the previous step, the teacher should make sure the children can demonstrate understanding through their own actions. These may be more difficult because the phrases usually are a bit more abstract for youngsters. It is very important for some children to have many experiences related to these verbs. Various children and even the teacher may disagree about inclusive and exclusive categories. There are no absolutes. For example, as shown in Figure 6–12, some pupils may give good reasons for indicating that butterflies do go to school (especially if they have seen samples of some in a science lesson). Allow children to construct organizers based on their experiences and their reasoning.

PROCESS VERBS

All the verbs taught up to this point have been action verbs. The process verbs described here also involve activity, but the agent is not identified in the relationship. In these verb organizers, the relationship between the verb and the noun is that of process-patient. The noun acts as a patient in that something is happening to it. The noun does not initiate the action on its own. For example, in the sentence, "Glasses break," the relationship between the verb and noun is that of process-patient. The activity happens to the glass—the glasses do not initiate their own breaking. Something or someone not stated in the sentence initiates the action. Many young children seem to use process-patient relationships in place of action-agent relationships as a type of defense mechanism. For example, a child is likely to say, "The glass broke," rather than "I broke the glass." The process-patient relationship (the glass broke) would seem to be a transformation of the more basic relationship (I broke the glass) constructed for the purpose of avoiding guilt.

The verb "break" can have both an action and a process relationship with nouns at the same time. For example, in the sentence, "Waiters break glasses," the relationship of "waiters" and "break" is that of action-agent while the relationship of "glasses" and "break" is that of process-patient. The relationships stressed in this section are process-patient with the subject as the patient and the verb as process. Figure 6–13 involves a process verb and nouns acting as patients.

These verb organizers, as with previous ones, should be learned initially through actions—and also through pictures, films, etc. A good way of reinforcing these

Figure 6–12
Venturing into
Indirect Objects
(Locatives)

Girls go to school. Boys go to school. Teachers go to school. Butterflies don't go to school.

actions is through the use of videotapes. When demonstrating these verbs, the teacher videotapes the activity, then asks the pupils to describe the actions they view using nouns with the verbs. Or, the teacher might show a child a card with the words "volcanoes explode." The child would need to identify the appropriate activity on a videotape.

This type of verb organizer is particularly adaptable to very elementary science experiments because the nouns involved in the relationships can be inanimate. In contrast, action-agent relationships almost always involve animate nouns.

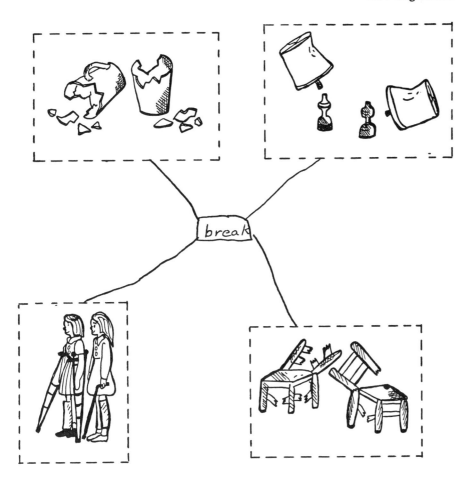

Figure 6–13
Verbs in the
Patient-Process
Relationship

Cups break. Lamps break. Chairs break. Legs break.

One popular science experiment involves the pupils' discovering things that float and things that do not. The activity can be based on direct experiences. The learners can experiment by placing objects in water. It is more stimulating if they attempt to guess whether or not an object will float before placing it in water. They then develop a verb organizer based on the results and write a summary of the experiment based on the verb organizer. Figure 6–14 is an example of such an experiment.

Figure 6–14
An Experiment
Unmuddies the
Water

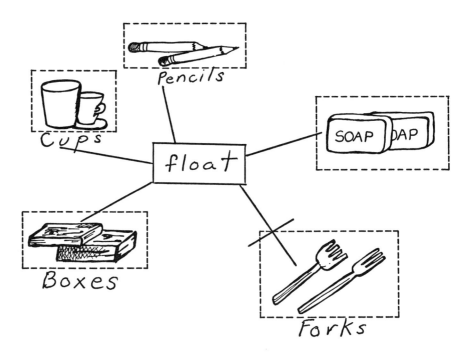

Following are some useful process verbs:

break
float
sink
explode
open
burn
melt

It must be remembered that if these are to be used in the process role in verb organizers, they must be related to a noun (usually inanimate) that does not initiate the action. The noun must represent something receiving the action.

Only plural nouns were used in the previous verb organizers in order to keep the verb consistent with the form first introduced. For example, the verb "run" was introduced as a verb of command. Later, in verb organizers, the same graphic form (although not the same function) was used. The third person plural form of the verb "run" has the same graphic form as the imperative form.

In singular nouns, the semantic relationships remain but the verb usually changes, most often by adding an "s." For example, in the sentence, "The baby sleeps," an "s" is added to the verb because the subject of the sentence is singular. Agreement of verb and subject in number (plural or singular) is not a semantic issue; it is more a grammatical one. Semantic organizers describe semantic relationships, not grammatical issues such as subject-verb agreement.

The organizer in Figure 6–15 begins to make a distinction between semantic relationships and grammatical issues. The verb in the semantic organizer does not end in "s." However, the student can learn that when writing a sentence in which the subject is singular, the "s" is added at the end. The important distinction between

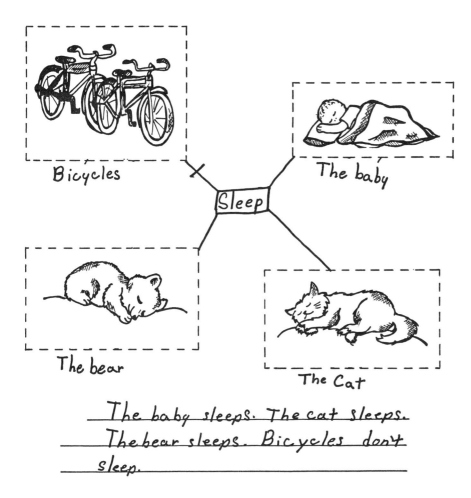

Figure 6–15
Singular Nouns
Provide a New
Element

semantics and syntax begins to be emphasized at this point. The teacher should use a plural subject for the exclusive category so that ''don't'' can be used appropriately.

INFERRED VERBS

Another type of verb organizer involves the use of two different verbs. This organizer can be an introduction to inference drawing. The exclusive category is inferred without being written in the organizer. For example, in the verb organizer in Figure 6–16, the cat is an exclusive category in relation to the verb ''play'' because in

Figure 6–16
The Two Verb
Organizer

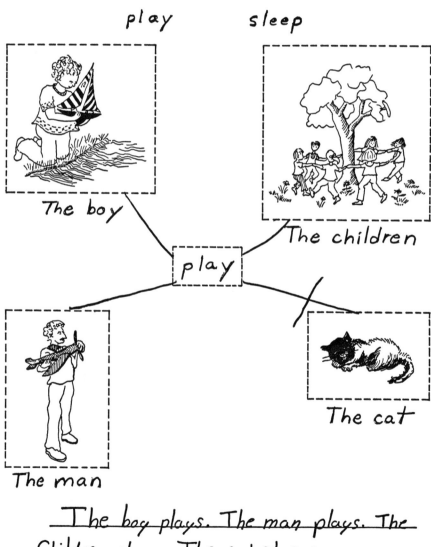

The boy plays. The man plays. The Children play. The cat sleeps.

The boy paints. The father paints. The girl paints. The mother cleans.

Figure 6–17
A Reverse Activity

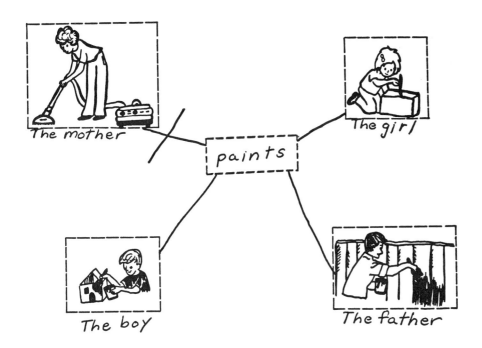

the picture the cat is not playing; it is sleeping. Therefore the cat is an inclusive category in relation to the verb "sleep."

As with all semantic organizers, the reverse activity should be taught as soon as possible. Figure 6–17 is a reverse activity in which the learner develops the semantic organizer based on the paragraph.

Many materials young children are expected to read use an auxiliary verb in conjunction with another verb. The word "can" has a rather subtle meaning that indicates a potential or an actual ability. Pictures, films, and direct experiences can help pupils understand the meaning of this auxiliary verb. Students should be led to realize that common nouns are not capitalized within sentences. The verb organizer shown in Figure 6–18 uses pictures of animals that have the potential to jump but are not shown in the act of jumping.

'CAN' AND 'CAN'T'

Figure 6–18
The Verb
Acquires an
Auxiliary

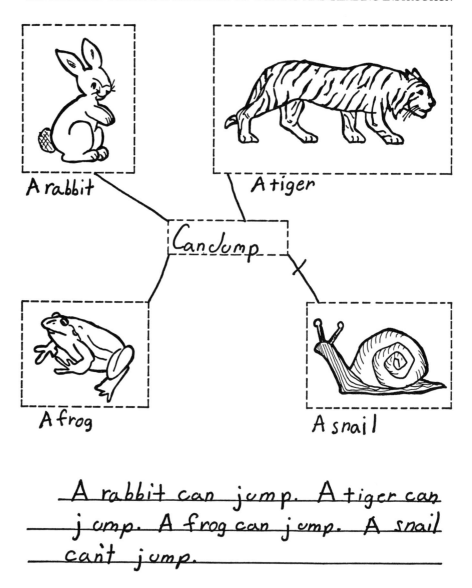

A rabbit can jump. A tiger can jump. A frog can jump. A snail can't jump.

COMPOUND (CONJOINED) SUBJECTS

The repetition of the same sentence patterns is important for establishing basic linguistic understandings. However, in normal writing, subjects often are conjoined. Figure 6–19, based on a verb organizer, involves compound (or conjoined) subjects.

Conjoining subjects can be taught with all verb organizers. Pupils also can be taught to use commas and the word "and" at this time. Many activities should involve developing verb organizers from paragraphs. In this way, pupils will be developing the understanding of how compound subjects relate to a verb.

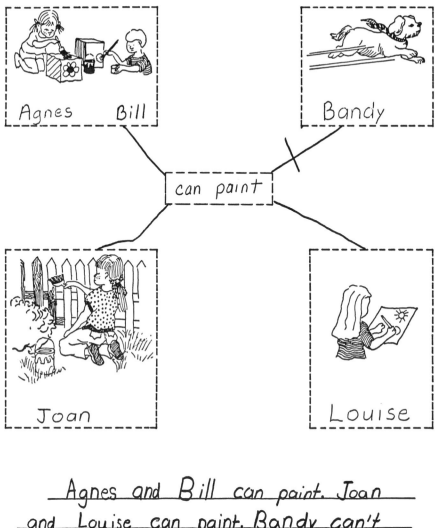

Figure 6–19
Compound, or
Conjoined,
Subjects

Agnes and Bill can paint. Joan and Louise can paint. Bandy can't paint.

'BUT'

For purposes of style, but for other reasons as well, the disjunctive "but" can be introduced with verb organizers. This disjunctive indicates that what follows is different from preceding ideas. The word "but" can be used to introduce the sentence representing the exclusive category, as shown in Figure 6–20.

Pupils will need to be alerted to the lack of a capital on the noun following the word "but." Sentence boundaries (capitals and marks of punctuation) should be empha-

Figure 6–20
The Disjunctive
Offers Variety

Helen and Sam can work.
Marie, Janet, and Arnold can work.
But Bobby can't work.

sized for they help to represent the organization of ideas. Some pupils may need special help in understanding why and when upper-case and lower-case letters are used.

BENE-FACTIVE VERBS

Benefactive verb organizers always involve a verb phrase that includes both the verb and a direct object. These verbs designate some kind of possession (or lack or less of it). These, as well as the state verbs discussed in the next section, are difficult for some language-disabled children. If pupils do not succeed in creating organizers with benefactive verbs, the teacher should move quickly away from them and come back later.

"Have" is an example of a benefactive verb. It is particularly useful for describing parts of the body. (See Figure 6–21.) A number of verb organizers and paragraphs can

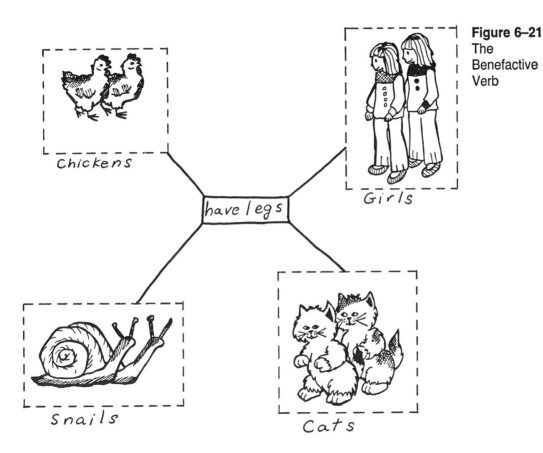

Figure 6–21
The Benefactive Verb

Chickens have legs. Girls have legs. Cats have legs. Snails don't have legs.

be developed based on science and social studies projects. Here are some useful benefactive verbs:

have	(arms)
get	(sick)
want	(toys)
need	(money)
lose	(antlers)
take	(medicine)
steal	(food)
borrow	(sugar)

STATE VERBS   The most common state verb is "to be" in its various forms. It should not be taught in isolation. It will be remembered best if it is taught as a complete verb phrase (with accompanying noun or adjective) because, in that way, it represents more meaning. Adjectives can be introduced as in Figure 6–22.

Figure 6–22
A Use of the
Verb 'To Be'

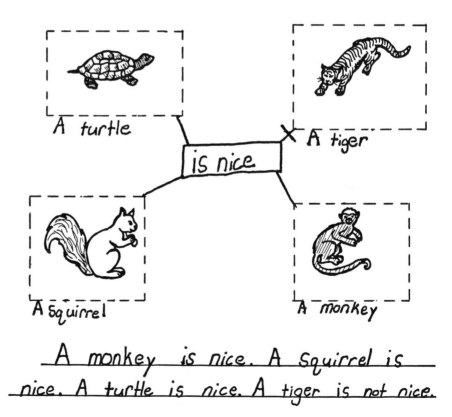

A turtle   A tiger

is nice

A Squirrel   A monkey

A monkey is nice. A Squirrel is nice. A turtle is nice. A tiger is not nice.

Pupils writing paragraphs must be given careful instruction on the exclusive category. They will need a good deal of practice in placing the "not" after the verb and before the adjective. They will need to understand that this negative form replaces the "don't" in previous verb organizers. Forms of "to be" also can be used for categorizing activities, such as in Figure 6–23.

"To be" is not the only verb to express state. Verbs and verb phrases such as "live in," "stay," "wait," etc., also express state. Locatives (designators of location) can be taught along with the state verbs. The verb organizer in Figure 6–24 is an example.

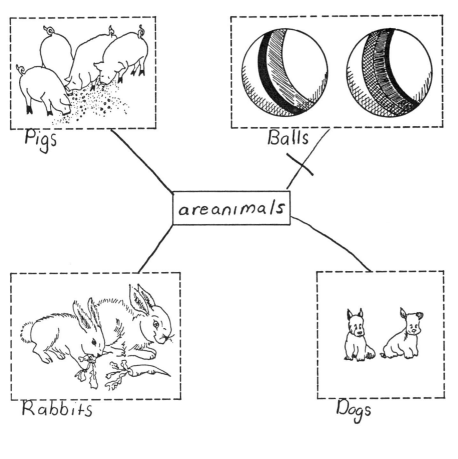

Figure 6–23
Categorizing
Activities

Pigs are animals. Rabbits are animals. Dogs are animals. Balls are not animals. Ball are toys.

Figure 6–24
Locatives as
Verb Enhancers

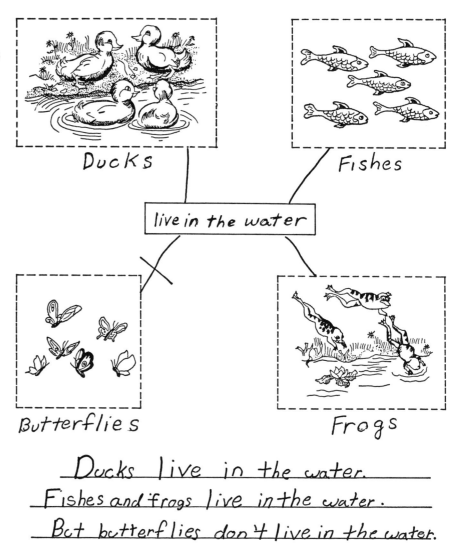

Ducks live in the water.
Fishes and frogs live in the water.
But butterflies don't live in the water.

GENERAL-
IZING VERBS

As a review and internalization of the functions of the varied types of verbs, the teacher should direct the children to "generalize" verbs in a game format (see Figure 6–25). First, the children are asked to write three specific verbs (dictated by the teacher) at the top of a page. (These verbs should have been learned as part of the spelling program.) Below the verbs, the pupils develop an organizer with, say, eight nouns around an empty verb box. At this point, they should not draw perpendicular (excluding) lines. The teacher develops the identical organizer on the chalkboard.

The teacher now takes a card with one of the verbs written on it from a box but does not show it to the pupils. The teacher draws lines at right angles across the lines

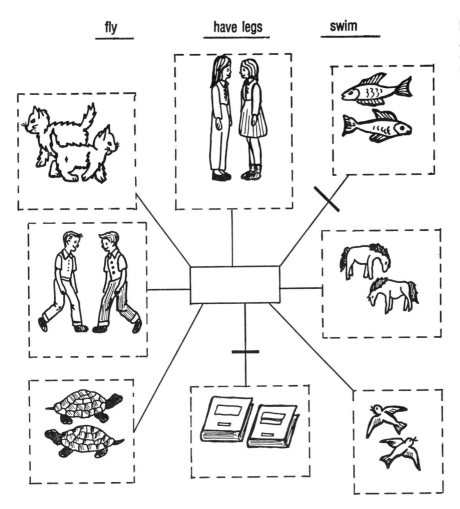

Figure 6–25
A Game for
Generalizing
Verbs

connecting the inappropriate nouns to the verb box and the children do so as well. Now the pupils must guess the verb.

For example, if the verb taken from the box is "have legs," the teacher would draw the perpendicular or excluding lines across the lines connecting fishes and books to the verb box. Pupils then guess by trial and error which word was drawn from the box. Children may have their chances to draw words from the box and to play with new verbs. The game serves as a review as well as a readiness activity for extended work of this nature.

As work proceeds with the various types of verb organizers and as learners become familiar enough with the written forms of a number of verbs and nouns, the teacher may want to help the class develop verb organizers without pictures. In that case, the verb in lower-case letters (without picture) is placed in a center box and the children

VERB ORGANIZERS WITHOUT PICTURES

Figure 6–26
Ta-dah! Look,
Ma, No
Pictures!

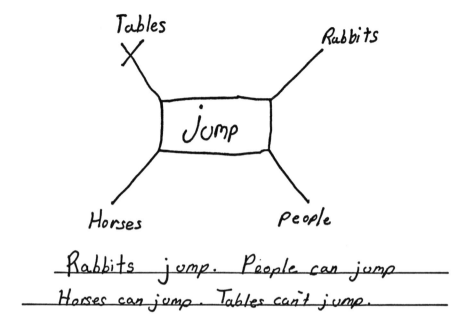

place related nouns at the ends of as many arms extending from the box as desired or needed.

This should begin with plural verbs and nouns. All nouns should be capitalized if the students are to write stories based on the verb organizer. Figure 6–26 is an example of a simple verb organizer without pictures plus the story organized from it by a first grader who had not written more than a word or two earlier.

CONCLUSION   The steps presented in this chapter have helped many learners experience their first success in composing. However, teachers may want to change the order because the nature of a child's experiences are different from those discussed here. In general, it seems profitable to begin with verb organizers involving action verbs. Teachers may want to add types of verb organizers not depicted in the chapter.

As a result of working with verb organizers, pupils should be able to comprehend and write simple paragraphs. They also should have developed a vocabulary of hundreds of words, including verbs, nouns, adjectives, and conjunctions. Most importantly, they will have a basic understanding of how language works and will be prepared to read in books.

Chapter 7

Noun Organizers

Noun organizers emphasize the noun, rather than the verb, as the central word. In noun organizers the first letter of the noun is capitalized and placed in the central position, with a variety of verbs (starting with lower-case letters) surrounding it. Noun organizers help children learn to read and write paragraphs similar to those found in books that feature factual information. They are useful for introducing summarizing, comparing/contrasting, and generalizing. Noun organizers also help children develop questioning strategies.

THE GENESIS OF NOUN ORGANIZERS

Noun organizers usually are based on the learner's understanding of verb organizers. However, some children in first or second grade may start with noun organizers if they appear to have developed sufficient knowledge of subject-predicate relationships. For those who previously learned verb organizers, the teacher will need to point out how they differ from noun organizers.

In verb organizers the relationships of the nouns to the verb within sentences basically remain the same so when pupils write a paragraph, the syntactic structures of the sentences remain consistent. The same basic patterns are repeated in each sentence in the paragraph. However, it is important also to teach the use of a greater variety of sentences within a single paragraph. Noun organizers introduce sentences which more directly approximate those found in basal readers and other textbooks.

Verbs (and nouns) are central to the sentence but a noun normally represents an idea that is central to the paragraph. The noun organizer emphasizes the development of a paragraph in which the noun represents the central topic and the verbs the comments regarding that topic.

MODELING

Noun organizers, as with all semantic organizers, should be based on experiences. If the topic is to be an animal, children should observe the animal. For example, if elephants are to be the topic of a noun organizer, the pupils should observe one or more elephants, either at a zoo or in films. Films probably are better than film strips because they show action—and verbs of action, to begin with, remain important in noun organizers.

The teacher then develops a noun organizer with elephants as the topic in the center box (see Figure 7–1). By this time, the youngsters should not need a picture along with the noun. However, if a picture is helpful, then one with more than one elephant should be used. Initially, plural nouns are developed. The teacher asks the learners to describe the action performed by the elephants. These verbs then are clustered around the noun. One verb usually is an exclusive category, indicating that the animal does not perform that activity.

A child may suggest that Dumbo, the flying elephant, belongs in the organizer and is not an exclusive item. Such differences in thinking are inevitable since children's views on the world are often constructed differently from one another and from those of the teacher. Differences should be discussed. The teacher may want to differentiate between fantasy and reality or allow a child to organize as the child sees fit, dependent upon the purpose of the lesson.

Based on the noun organizer, the teacher models the paragraph. Children usually require special help here. At first, they may reverse the verb and noun in the sentences because they are basing word order on previously learned verb organizers. In order to write a paragraph based on a verb organizer, pupils write the nouns on each "leg" of

Figure 7–1
Construction of a Basic Noun Organizer

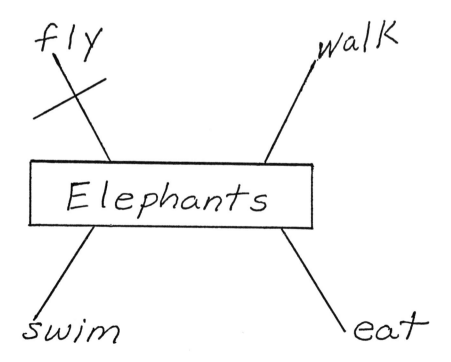

the organizer, and each noun becomes the first word of a sentence, all using the verb in the middle box. With noun organizers the noun is in the middle box and the verbs are on the "legs." The noun is the first word followed by a different verb in each sentence.

At this point, it sometimes is helpful if the pupils learn to draw two lines under the verb, both in semantic organizers and in paragraphs. This helps them identify the differences between nouns and verbs and thus develop a better sense of standard word order in sentences. Writing the nouns in capitals also gives the youngsters a clue to word order if they have begun to internalize sentence boundary rules. Figure 7–2 is an example of one child's organizer.

VARYING VERB TYPES

As children mature in language, they learn to deal with a variety of verb types within a context. Noun organizers lend themselves to varieties of noun-verb relationships within a single paragraph. As in the development of verb organizers, the pupils should learn to write a paragraph based on a noun organizer before attempting to develop a noun organizer based on a paragraph. The activity of writing the paragraph helps to internalize the schema involved in understanding the relationships and regularities of language.

Figure 7–3 demonstrates a noun organizer making use of a variety of verb-noun relationships.

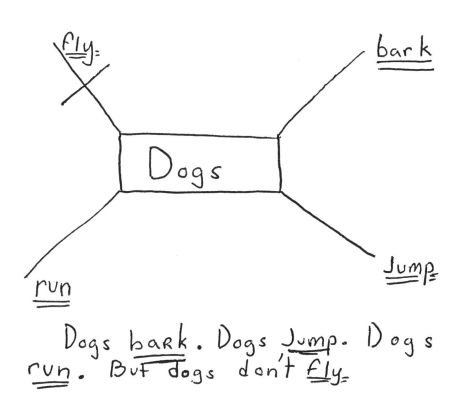

Figure 7–2
How One Child
Created a Noun
Organizer

Figure 7–3
Noun Organizer
with Nouns and
Verbs

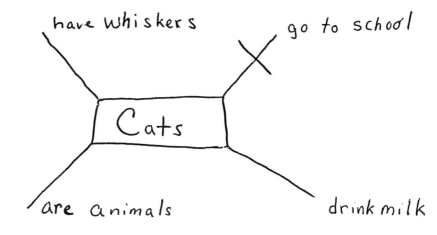

REVERSING THE PROCESS   As with verb organizers, pupils should be taught to reverse the process by developing a semantic organizer based on a prepared paragraph. Children will transfer what they learn more readily if the teacher consistently emphasizes the construction of organizers for both writing and reading. At almost every opportunity, pupils should construct organizers based on their paragraph reading after they have learned to write paragraphs based on organizers. (See Figure 7–4.)

Figure 7–4
Paragraph-
Based
Organizer

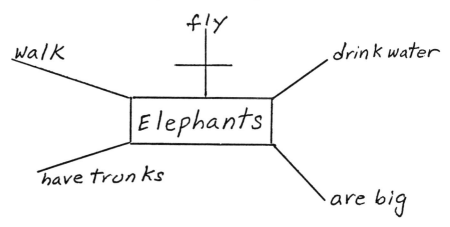

The next step is to teach rewriting with the goal of introducing summarizing. **REWRITING**
Summarizing involves rewriting an author's major ideas without rewriting all of the
exact words in the same sentence patterns. At this point the children are not truly
summarizing. But they are not merely copying, either, even though their words and
sentences will resemble the authors'.

The pupil develops a noun organizer based on a paragraph, then writes a paragraph
based on the organizer. This is similar to using verb organizers. However, here
children are taught to eliminate what they consider less important information.
Eliminating the unimportant is a vital task in learning, and is particularly essential for
summarizing. In Figure 7–5, the pupil eliminated the first sentence because it was
relatively unimportant to the other facts. The child also was asked to include only four
facts, although there are seven in the paragraph.

Figure 7–5
Rewriting and
Condensing

These are fishes. Fishes swim.
Fishes blow bubbles. Fishes eat
worms. Fishes have fins. But fishes
don't run. Fishes don't have ears.

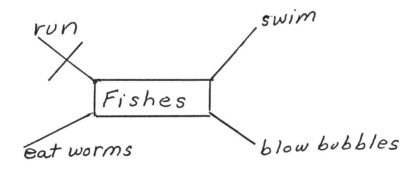

**COMPARING
AND
CONTRAST-
ING**

Based on rather simple noun organizers, a child can be taught to compare and contrast two animals or objects. Noun organizers provide the basic tool for this rather complex process. Many young children will be ready to perform this task after they have learned the preceding activities thoroughly. Others may not be ready even then. The way to determine the pupils' capabilities is to try this type of exercise. If they cannot (or do not) learn, then perhaps they are not ready yet.

In this series of tasks the youngsters learn to write a paragraph in which the likeness and differences of two animals or things are described. Again, this must be based on experience. The example in Figure 7–6 compares frogs and toads. The learners first

Figure 7–6
Noun Organizer
for Frogs

This is a frog. Frogs have wet skin. Frogs have smooth skin. Frogs jump fast. Frogs jump far. Frogs live on land. Frogs live in water too.

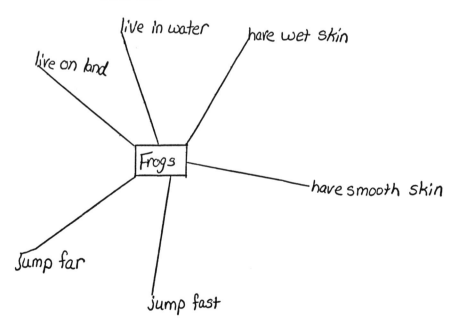

Figure 7–7
Noun Organizer
for Toads

This is a toad. Toads have dry
skin. Toads have rough skin. Toads
don't jump far. Toads don't jump high.
Toads don't jump fast. Toads live on
land. Toads live in water too.

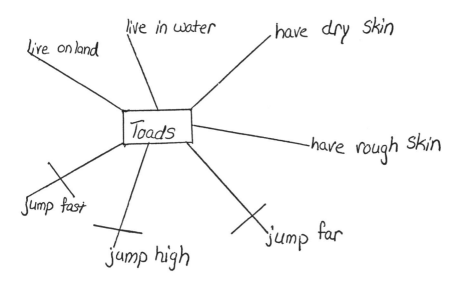

develop a noun organizer based on the paragraph describing frogs. The children next
develop a noun organizer based on the paragraph describing toads. (See Figure 7–7.)

At this point the pupils learn how to reorganize for comparing and contrasting. In
the reorganized diagram the information that is the same for both toads and frogs is
removed from each noun organizer and placed between them. The information true
for only one of the noun organizers (frog or toad) remains. Lines are drawn from each
organizer to the common information. The pupils then write a paragraph in which
frogs and toads are contrasted and compared. Figure 7–8 is one youngster's result.

Figure 7–8
Comparing and
Contrasting
Frogs and
Toads

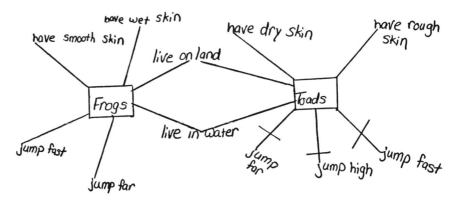

Frogs have wet skin. Frogs have smooth
skin. Frogs jump fast. Frogs jump far.

Toads have dry skin. Toads have rough skin.
Toads don't jump fast. Toads don't jump high. Toads
don't jump far.

Frogs and toads live on land. Frogs and
toads live in water.

CONCLUSION   Only a few patterns of noun organizers are demonstrated in this chapter. Noun
organizers using all of the verb types and more (described in Chapter 6) can be
developed. These simple noun patterns are important as they lay the groundwork for
more complex organizations later. They are particularly effective in helping children
organize for writing and reading about a simple topic. Another important use is tied to
comprehension when pupils are asked to construct a noun organizer based on
something they have read.

Teachers should keep in mind that these noun organizers are suitable for expository
or informational writing patterns that develop comments (subordinate ideas) around a
topic (superordinate idea). In Chapter 9, where episodic organizers are introduced,
pupils focus on story (narrative) and sequential patterns.

Chapter 8

Concept Organizers

Concept organizers, based on brainstorming and telegraphic language, permit more creative thinking and language structuring than previous semantic organizers. However, they are rooted in the basic organizational patterns learned earlier. Concept organizers are extremely adaptable and are applicable to many uses in preorganizing and postorganizing ideas for reading and writing. They are useful from first grade through college as organizational tools for planning writing, predicting what is to be read, and ascertaining comprehension of written discourse.

ROOTS OF CONCEPT ORGANIZERS

In the preceding semantic organizers, semantic relationships and syntactic structures were basically the same. For example, in both verb and noun organizers, two words such as "frog" and "jump" can be related semantically, with the resulting syntax: "Frogs jump." The pupil was able to write sentences and paragraphs (syntactic structures) using the same words as in the semantic relationship.

In concept organizers these relationships are less likely to be controlled; they involve more creative language processes. The major difference between the noun organizer and concept organizer, at least on the surface, is that the latter uses telegraphic language (just the essential key words), whereas the noun organizer involves the entire verb phrase. A comparison of noun and concept organizers is shown in Figure 8–1. The topic of horses is organized first in terms of a noun organizer; then, with telegraphic language, the same relationships are demonstrated in the concept organizer.

As indicated, the noun organizer involves the use of a full syntactic frame, the concept organizer the fewest words necessary to retain concept meanings. Because telegraphic language is used, the concept organizer is a more adaptable and more useful tool than either the verb or noun organizer. In a sense the other types of organizers were preparations for the concept organizer. Through the use of concept

Figure 8–1
Noun and
Concept
Organizers
Compared

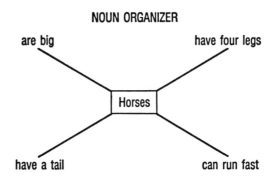

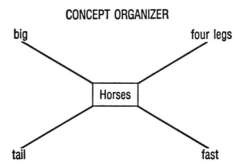

organizers, children learn to organize ideas at a semantic level as an activity apart from structuring sentences (syntax).

In developing concept organizers, the teacher gradually helps students use only those words essential to the understanding of the semantic relationships. By using fewer words in the semantic organizers, the semantic relationships and syntactic structures begin to separate. This separation helps students to organize their thoughts as tasks aside from sentence structuring. Once the ideas are organized, the pupils can concentrate on syntax without worrying about becoming disorganized or forgetting the ideas.

**BASIC
PROCEDURES**
The teacher can elicit ideas from students about a topic and construct a concept organizer that does not contain all the syntactic information found in noun organizers. (See Figure 8–2.) A variety of syntactic structures can be developed based on this one concept organizer. The following sample was written by a first grader:

> Spiders are not insects. Spiders are little animals. Spiders have eight legs. Spiders make silk webs. Spiders kill bugs. Spiders help farmers. Sometimes spiders are dangerous.

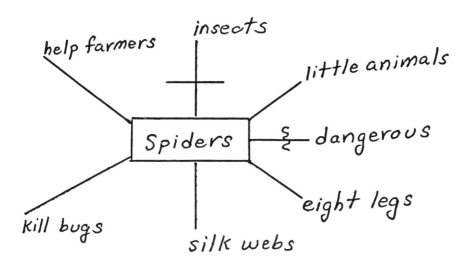

Figure 8–2
Construction of
a Concept
Organizer

Another more mature way of expressing the relationships in the concept organizer was written by a third grade child:

> Spiders are not insects. They are little animals. They have eight legs and make silk webs. They help farmers because they kill bugs. Some spiders can be dangerous.

At this point, pupils should be encouraged to develop concept organizers based on a paragraph. The paragraph in Figure 8–3 was developed by a first grader into a concept organizer.

Pupils may need a great deal of help in deciding which words are important and which can be omitted; however, it is worth the effort. Proficient reading is selective. Good reading involves understanding what words contribute most to a topic or major idea. Some children seem to need specific help in understanding that some words may be omitted yet the basic meaning may be retained. To reinforce telegraphic language of the concept organizer, it is helpful for the pupils to reconstruct many of the previously learned noun organizers as concept organizers. After practice with telegraphic language the youngsters can learn to write original and creative compositions.

Creative writing should be introduced solely on the basis of original ideas. The teacher then can help pupils write a paragraph. Figure 8–4 represents such a task, written by a first grader.

It should be expected that, in the beginning, many youngsters will create stilted sentence patterns, as in this example. However, early attempts should not be overcorrected. Learners should be encouraged to produce more original paragraphs based on concept organizers.

Figure 8–3
A First Grader's
Concept
Organizer

Crabs live in the ocean. Crabs have legs. Crabs have strong claws. Crabs have hard shells. Crabs eat dead fish.

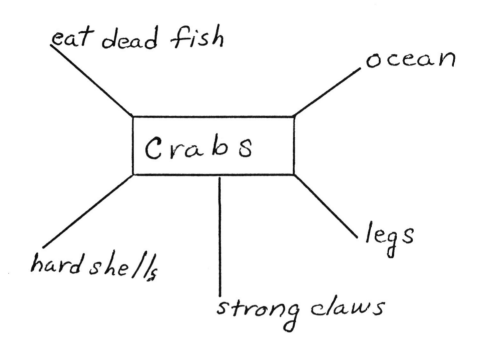

**INTRO-
DUCING
PRONOUNS**

Pronouns are difficult, particularly for children who have special language needs. For example the word "it" may appear four times in a single paragraph and have three or four different meanings. At this point, teachers should not attempt to demonstrate how to deal with the various subtleties involving pronouns; instead, they should begin with pronouns that consistently refer to the same noun.

"They" is introduced first by indicating that the repetition of the same word (the topic) at the beginning of each sentence can be boring. That repeated word can be changed to a pronoun. The teacher demonstrates this by using a previously developed paragraph such as the one about "friends" in Figure 8–4. Under the word "Friends" in the center box of the organizer, the teacher writes the word "They" (with initial capital letter).

The teacher models this by rewriting the paragraph beginning with the word "Friends" for the first sentence and "They" to start the other sentences. It should be

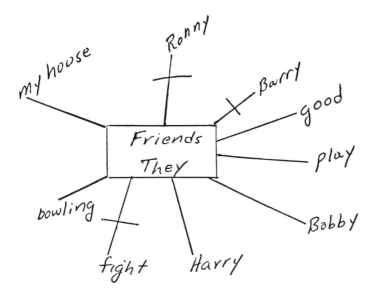

Figure 8–4
A First Grader's
Creative Writing

Friends are good. They play. They are Bobby and Harry. They don't fight. They go bowling. Friends come to my house. Friends are not Ronny and Barry.

emphasized to the pupils that the paragraph has the same meaning when "They" replaces "Friends." Children should be encouraged to practice this by writing many paragraphs using a singular subject that takes such a neuter pronoun. Variations may be developed by demonstrating that the noun topic may be repeated at the beginning of the last sentence. Some paragraphs can be written with the noun and pronoun alternating as the beginning word in every other sentence.

**AUTOBI-
OGRAPHIES
AND
BIOGRAPHIES**

The writing of autobiographies and biographies helps to develop the use of personal pronouns. The personal pronoun ''I'' is used for the autobiography and ''He'' or ''She'' for biographies of classmates or other persons. The teacher needs to help children structure such types of writing.

One pupil may be selected to model this activity. The child can construct an organizer on the chalkboard with ''I'' in the center while the teacher also constructs one with the child's name and ''He'' or ''She'' (note capitals) in the center. For example, Danny wrote ''I'' in the center of his organizer and the teacher wrote ''Danny'' and ''He'' in hers. Danny would be writing an autobiography while the teacher and the class were writing a biography about Danny. The teacher then asked Danny for information about himself and, using telegraphic language, constructed the concept

Figure 8–5
A Third
Grader's Auto-
biography

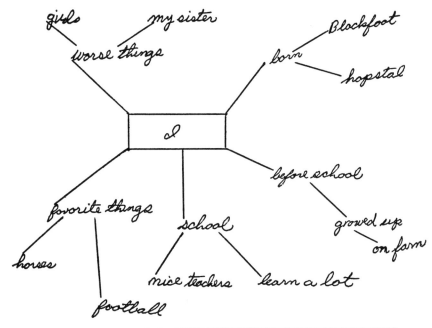

I was borned in a hopstal in Blackfoot. Before I wentd to school I growed big on a farm. I learn a lot at school and I have nice teachers. My favorite things are football and horses. My worstes thing is girls and the really worstes thing in the hole world is my sister.

organizer. The class copied the teacher's organizer and Danny constructed his own. Later, the teacher modeled the paragraph. Each youngster should attempt to develop an autobiography using the same form of the organizer. This activity can be extended by interviewing other pupils and adults, followed by the writing of biographies.

Harry, a third grader, was asked to write an autobiography about where he was born, what happened before school, what school was like, and what were his favorite and least-liked things. Harry formulated this concept organizer and wrote a paragraph. (See Figure 8–5.) He then was asked to use a similar format to write, not about himself but about another youngster in the class, and he wrote about Sharon (a girl!). (See Figure 8–6.) His noticeable improvement seemed to come about from practice alone.

Figure 8–6
The Same Third Grader Tries Biography

Sharon was born in Burley. Her favorite things are making pot holders and riding the exccalator in stores. Her most favorite thing is Bobby and he lives down the street. Sharon wants to be a cheerleader and a airplane stewardess. Sharon had vacations in Jackson, and California and Chubbuck.

Once Harry had enough practice in writing biographies about other youngsters in the class, he was asked to write those of his family, his parents, and his grandparents. Figure 8–7 is an example of Harry's biography of his great-grandfather, based on information supplied by his grandmother. In that example, Harry's spelling and language have further improved.

Figure 8–7
The Same Third Grader's Improvement in Biography

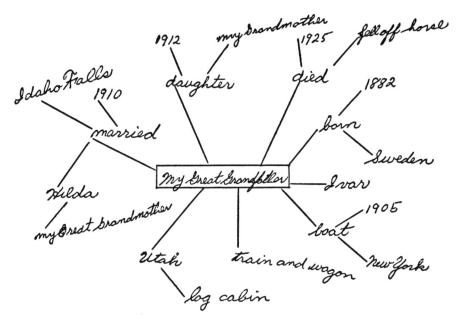

My Great Grandfather was born in 1882 in Sweden. His name was Ivar. He took a boat to New York in 1905. Then he took a wagon and a train. He went to Utah and he built a log cabin. Then he married my Great Grandmother in 1910. Her name was Hilda. They got married in Idaho Falls. Then in 1912 they had a daughter. She got to be my Grandmother. My Great Grandfather died in 1925. He fell off a horse.

Using the same type of biography organizer, Harry was able to write a biography of an inanimate object—in this case, a chair. (See Figure 8–8.)

A great deal of creativity can be developed using this biographical approach with concept organizers. When first using them for biographies, a teacher might pre-organize the information by writing subheadings to initiate questions regarding where and when youngsters were born, where they lived, and their interests. However, another approach, leading to more creative discoveries, involves asking youngsters to gather information through a "semantic collector." Here they "empty out their heads" and get the ideas down in any random order. (See Figure 8–9.) The youngsters then are asked to regroup and reorganize that information. (See Figure 8–10.)

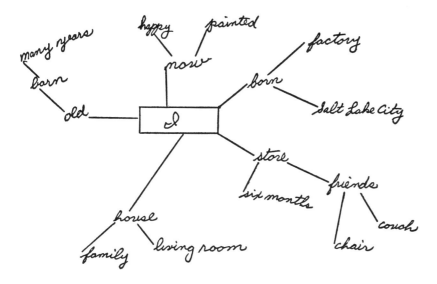

Figure 8–8
A Biography of—a Chair!

I was born in a factory in Salt Lake City. I lived in a store for six months. I had two good friends. One friend was a chair, and the other was a couch. Then one day I moved to a house. The house had a big pretty living room. There was a nice family. Then I got old and people put me in a barn. I stayed there many years. Then a new family came. Now I am back in the living room and I am a happy chair because I am painted just like use to be.

Figure 8–9
Random
Assembly in a
Concept
Organizer

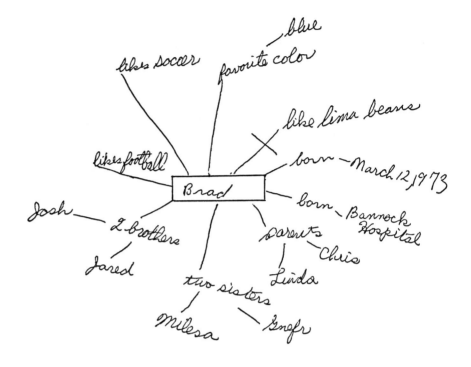

Figure 8–10
Random Ideas
Reorganized

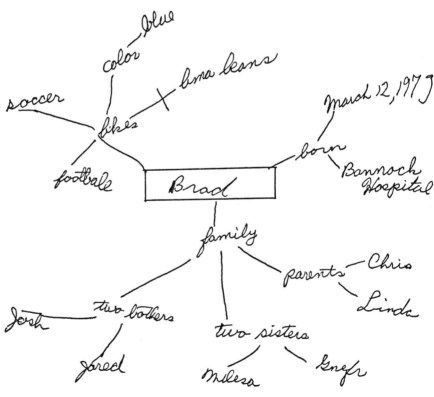

At this point the pupils will be able to write a biography that is well organized, possibly in three logical paragraphs. The three paragraphs are organized based on the categories: born, family, and likes.

Brad

Brad was born on March 12, 1973. He was born in Bannock Hospital.
Chris and Linda are his parents. He has two sisters named Milesa and Gnefr. He has two brothers named Jared and Josh.
He likes football and soccer. His favorite color is blue. He does not like lima beans.

Figure 8–11 is another "biography" in which the pupil (a third grader) personalized an inanimate object—a freezer refrigerator.

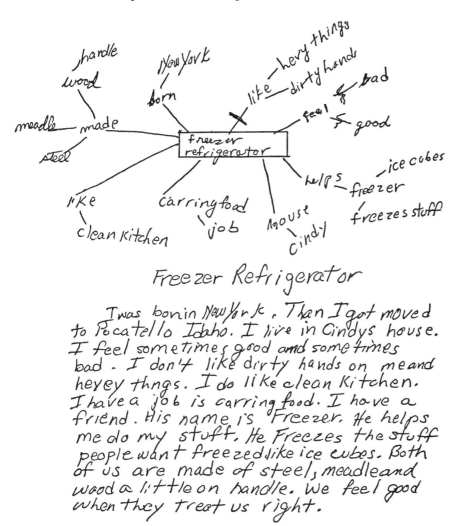

Figure 8–11
'Personalized'
Biography—of a
Freezer
Refrigerator

Pupils, through brainstorming, can construct very imaginative "biography" organizers. They can make up the names of new creatures by alternating the writing of consonants and vowels, like Chris's "padoxur." Chris describes his creature in Figure 8–12.

Another interesting and creative activity involves combining two animals into a new one, such as "dinophant," "rhinogator," or "hippohound." Pupils brainstorm ideas first with the teacher, other children, or on their own, then construct concept organizers. After the first draft of a biography is completed, peer conferencing—with or without teacher input—can help the students clarify ideas and syntax before they write a second or final draft. Through peer conferencing, children with similar interests and/or objectives help one another with their writing projects. (See Chapter 11 for more information about peer conferencing.)

Figure 8–12
Creative
Biography of a
'Padoxur'

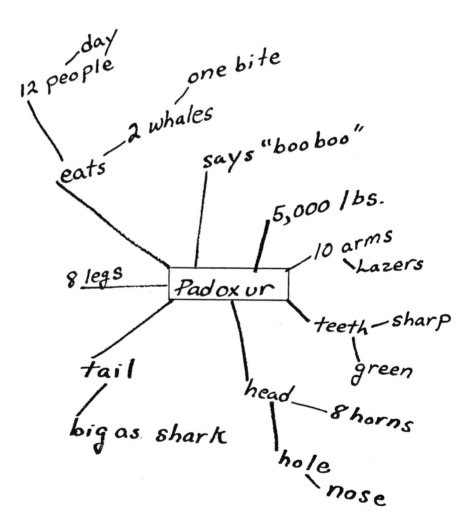

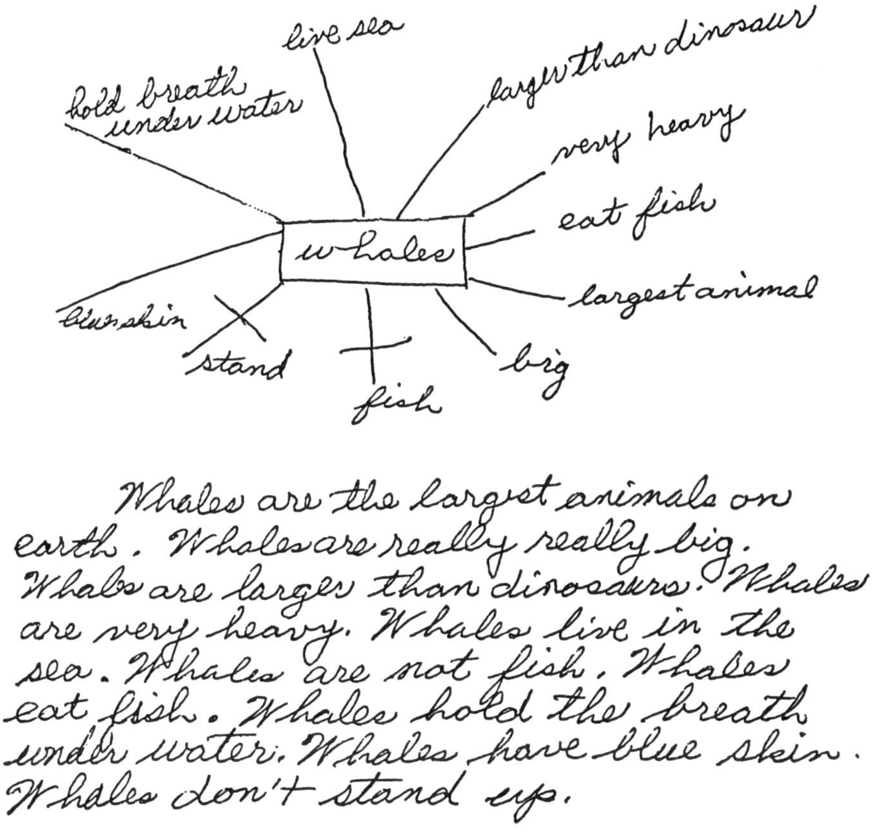
live sea
hold breath under water
larger than dinosaur
very heavy
eat fish
whales
largest animal
big
fish
stand
blue skin
Whales are the largest animals on earth. Whales are really really big. Whals are larger than dinosaurs. Whales are very heavy. Whales live in the sea. Whales are not fish. Whales eat fish. Whales hold the breath under water. Whales have blue skin. Whales don't stand up.

Figure 8–13
Summarizing

SUMMARIZING

Concept organizers also are tools for teaching pupils to read, gather information, and summarize. The teacher probably will need to offer considerable assistance in helping learners delete less important information. Some children practically recopy a passage because they have difficulty deciding what to leave out. One way to help them to summarize rather than to recopy is to limit the number of "legs" on the concept organizer. In the example in Figure 8–13 Arnold's original passage on whales had 20 sentences and the teacher limited the organizer to ten "legs."

Such concept organizers help pupils avoid copying because once they are developed with telegraphic language, the author's original syntax may be lost but the concepts and relationships are retained.

NEWS REPORTING

Youngsters can be taught to gather information about a particular topic by asking questions. One approach is to use pictures from newspapers, or magazines, or original drawings. One picture of an accident scene was helpful in teaching youngsters to ask questions, gather information, and write a news article. A lesson was

Figure 8–14
Using a Picture as Basis for a News Report Organizer

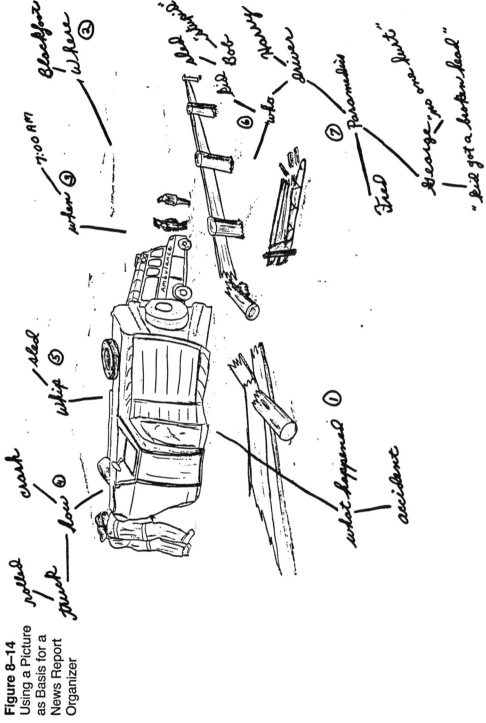

developed based upon the picture. The pupils were asked what they would do if they were television or newspaper reporters on the scene. They answered that they would have to ask questions. What questions would they ask? The organizer in Figure 8–14 was developed by Deena. Based on the organizer, Deena then prepared her script for a television news broadcast:

> Today we had an accident in Blackfoot on highway S.7. It happened at 7:00 a.m. The truck rolled over several times. Then it stopped. It happened because a sled was coming the other way. When the truck driver tried to stop it started to skid. The driver is Harry. He said, ''Stupid kid'' and got angry. The kid on the sled was Bob and he said, ''Stupid driver.'' The paramedics (Fred and George) said, ''The kid got a broken head but no one was seriously hurt. This is Deena for Newsbeat 8 saying, ''Drive safely.''

The ability to write more than one paragraph is based on organizational skills. The topic of each paragraph should be different yet related to the previous one. A two-paragraph composition can be developed using basic noun or concept clusters. For example, the teacher can discuss the topic of pets. Some children may have dogs or cats. The teacher may help the youngsters develop a concept organizer about each of these pets, then teach the pupils to write each paragraph separately. Indenting the beginning of each paragraph should be emphasized at this point. These two paragraphs can be extended into several paragraphs when other pets are introduced. Figure 8–15 represents an expanded concept organizer based on the topic of pets. Pupils can be taught to write five paragraphs based on this semantic organizer.

WRITING PARAGRAPHS

To write each paragraph, the youngsters need to attend to each organizer as if it were distinct from all others, beginning with the central organizer, then each extended one. The following composition evolved from such a semantic organizer. It was rewritten by a young child who was just starting to feel confident about any kind of written communication:

> Dogs are pets. Cats are pets. Birds are pets. Hamsters are pets.
>
> Dogs play. Dogs bark. Dogs jump. Dogs bite. Dogs eat dog food.
>
> Cats play. Cats meow. Cats jump. Cats scratch. Cats are cute.
>
> Birds jump. Birds are light. Birds fly. Birds eat seeds.
>
> Hamsters dig. Hamsters sleep. Hamsters run around. Hamsters are cute.

These five paragraphs also can be developed based on simple noun organizers. Young children usually feel a great sense of pride in the accomplishment of writing and understanding so much. More mature writers will use pronouns and conjoin some of the sentences.

Figure 8–15
Concept
Organizer as
Basis for
Paragraphs

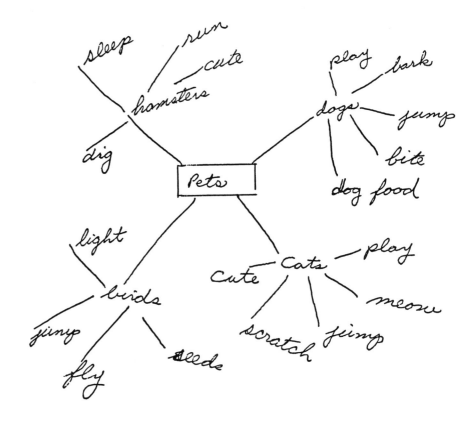

Pupils should be taught to reverse the operation and develop semantic organizers based on several paragraphs. In Figure 8–15, the pupil develops a crude composition based on an organizer. In Figure 8–16, a student developed an organizer based on the following five paragraphs:

Cars are machines. Airplanes are machines. Motorcycles are machines. Lawn mowers are machines.

Cars can go fast sometimes. They have four wheels. They drive on roads. They use gas.

Airplanes fly. They have wings. They go very fast sometimes. They land at airports.

Motorcycles have two wheels. They use gas. They climb hills. They have handle bars.

Lawn mowers cut grass. They go slow. They are noisy. They use gas.

Figure 8–16
Role Reversal:
Organizer is
Based on
Paragraphs

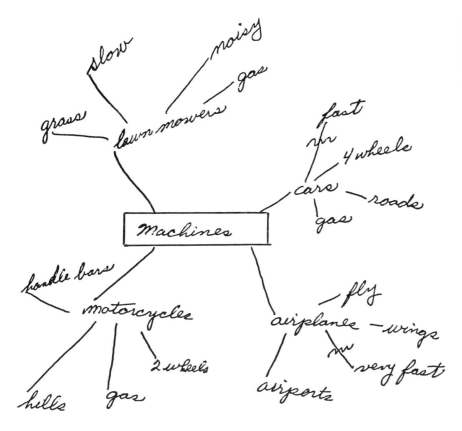

As demonstrated in Chapter 7 on noun organizers, youngsters can be taught to compare and contrast. Concept organizers are even more adaptable for developing comparisons and contrasts. For example, youngsters were taught to compare the similarities of and differences between moths and butterflies. First, they developed a concept organizer related to moths, then one on butterflies. These were combined into a comparative organizer. Pupils then wrote their stories in three paragraphs. Figures 8–17a, 8–17b, and 8–17c demonstrate the sequence through examples of children's work.

One teacher used this comparative/contrastive type of organizer to develop an awareness of the similarities of and differences between the students and a visiting infant a parent brought into the resource room. The children were excited about the infant and the teacher capitalized on this interest by having them develop the organizer in Figure 8–18.

COMPARING AND CONTRASTING

Figure 8–17a
Concept
Organizer on
Moths

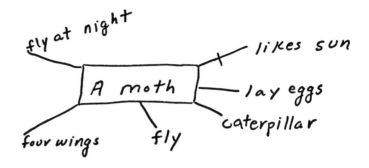

A moth

A moth lay eggs and comes from a caterpillar. A moth has four wings and can fly at night. A moth likes to fly at night but does not like the sun.

Figure 8–17b
Concept
Organizer on
Butterflies

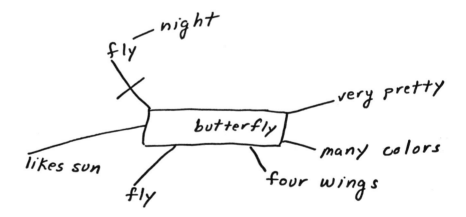

A butterfly is very pretty and it has many colors. A butterfly has four wings and it can fly. A butterfly likes the sun but it does not fly at night.

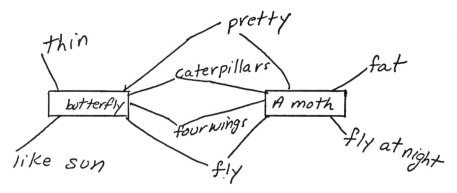

Figure 8–17c
A Comparison
Concept
Organizer

A butterfly is thin. It likes the sun.

A moth is fat. It likes to fly at night.

A butterfly and a moth fly. Both have four wings. Both come from caterpillars. Both are pretty.

It is not always necessary to write paragraphs. As in Figure 8–18, the organizer itself may be sufficient for such experiences. One of the values of the organizer is that it provides teachers with a tool to capitalize on interests that youngsters demonstrate at specific times.

RESEARCH STRATEGIES

Research, in this context, means teaching pupils to gather information from more than one source. The sequence starts with constructing a semantic collector, reorganizing that information into a concept organizer, and finally writing a short report based on the organizer.

For example, in one second grade science unit, children were learning about fish. The teacher asked them to gather information from different sources. The teacher gave them information through "resource people" who actually were characters drawn on large chart paper. The youngsters asked a fictitious character, Joe Hook, about his knowledge of fish—in particular, how fish were able to swim. Using a balloon procedure (as in cartoons and comic strips to portray words spoken by a character), Joe Hook told the children how fish were able to swim (see Figure 8–19).

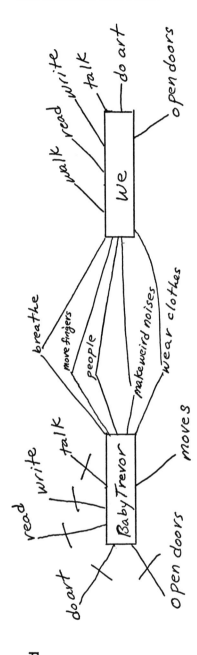

Figure 8–18
Similarities and
Differences in
the Same
Organizer

Figure 8–19
Debut of a
Resource
Person

However, when Joe Hook was asked how fish were able to stay upright without falling over, "he" was unable to supply the answer. So another character, also drawn on a large sheet of paper, was introduced and asked the question. This "resource person" was Mrs. Sinker, who supplied additional answers.

The pupils also found information in a picture in a book showing the fins on a fish. All of this information was gathered, collected on an organizer, then reorganized.

Figure 8–20
Information
Organized from
Research

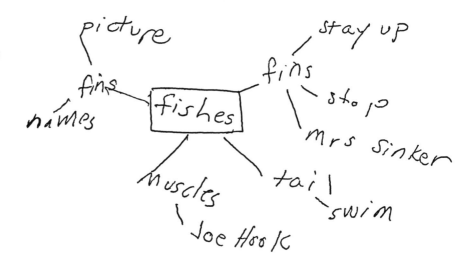

Mrs Sinker toled us how fishes swim. Fishes use theyr fins to stop and to stay up and to help them swim. Fishes use theyr tail to swim. Joe Hook toled us that fishes use they'r muscles to swim. We leaned the names of the fins from a picture.

(See Figure 8–20.) The youngsters could compare a paragraph about this information. They also could demonstrate within their paragraphs the sources of their information.

A sixth grade teacher used a more advanced approach in relation to insects. The pupils were asked to gather information about insects from several sources. Gerald used four books to do so. He demonstrated his sources of information by putting each author's name, date of book, and page number in parentheses. (See Figure 8–21.)

Some students, once they have grouped their information in a concept organizer, number each section in the order in which they will write paragraphs and even sentences in their reports. In extensive organizers in preparation for a detailed research report, the pupils may even label the parts of their organizers with Harvard Outline designations (I, A, 1, a, etc.). Used in this way, semantic organizers are an excellent introduction to formal outlining. Figure 8–22 is an example of one such organizer, done by a junior high school youngster, and is ready to be used as the base for a report.

Figure 8–21
Research in
more Advanced
Form

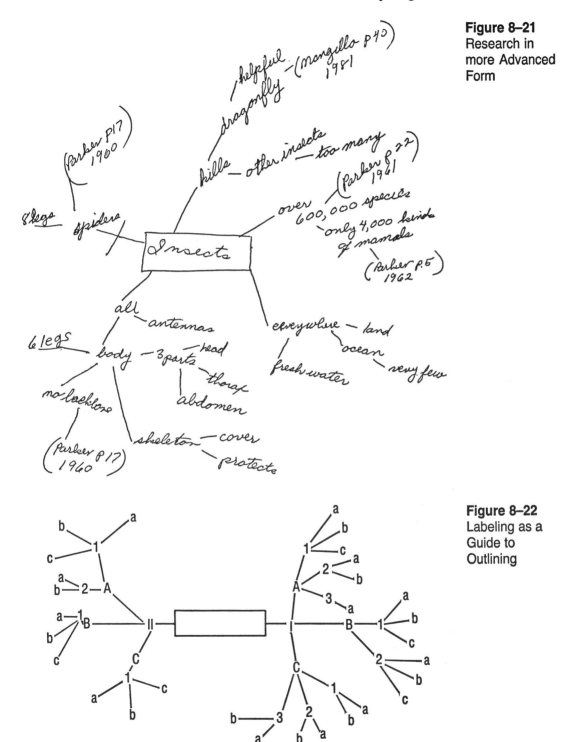

Figure 8–22
Labeling as a
Guide to
Outlining

Figure 8–23
The '20
Questions'
Concept
Organizer

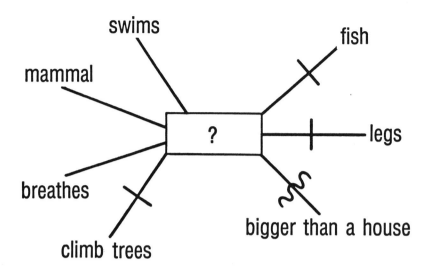

GENER-ALIZING THE TOPIC

Youngsters can be taught to generalize and discover the topic based upon the "20 Questions" game. It is useful for reviewing previously taught information, especially from a science or social studies unit. For this activity, the game is played in the following manner.

A rectangle is drawn on the board and a question mark is placed in it. The teacher might tell the students that the answer (the topic) is an animal studied in the science unit. The youngsters then develop questions about the topic. They can guess, for example, whether it has legs, or is bigger than a house, or climbs trees, or swims. The teacher can say "yes," "no," or "maybe." A "yes" reply is indicated by a "leg" on the organizer drawn in the usual way. A negative reply is represented by a crossed line, and a "maybe" or "sometimes" by a squiggly line across the line. The children can ask all kinds of questions and the teacher constructs the concept organizer. Figure 8–23 is an example of a concept organizer developed through the pupils' questioning.

POETRY WRITING

Poetry can be written using concept organizers. A pyramid poem can be written rather easily. Youngsters are asked to name a topic, or are given one, such as "spring." In the following example, youngsters were asked, "Tell me about spring." They said, "It's beautiful," and the teacher wrote "beautiful" in the center of the concept organizer. Asked for another idea, they responded that they could see many green plants. The teacher formed the concept organizer after receiving more ideas.

The teacher added a number in the box. That single word became the first line of the poem. The youngsters, with guidance, decided the order of the words in the poem and the teacher numbered each leg of the organizer to sequence the verse, as shown in Figure 8–24.

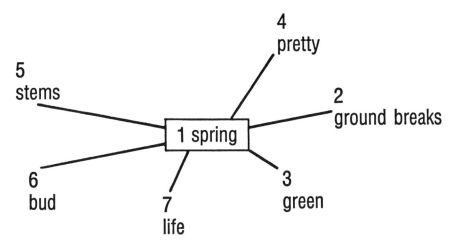

Figure 8–24
The Concept
Organizer Even
Writes Poetry

The children proceeded, with the teacher's guidance, to develop a poem using the same number of words as the number next to each word. For example, because spring was number 1, only one word was used in that line; because ground was number 2, only two words were used to tell about the ground, etc. The following poem was developed based on such an organizer:

Spring
Ground breaks
The green comes
All pretty things grow
Straight stems come up strong
A red bud ready to burst
A beautiful world comes forth to life

CONCLUSION

Concept organizers, as demonstrated, are adaptable to many situations and can be used for a multitude of tasks. They are useful for helping youngsters to organize their ideas before writing or reading, for summarizing after reading, and for organizing ideas from more than one source.

Concept organizers have great versatility. They can meet most challenges in organizing information related to content (factual) reading. Certainly not all of the possibilities have been explored in this chapter. Teachers will want to investigate additional ways of organizing ideas in relation to particular content areas.

The concept organizers examined in this chapter usually are not used to express relationships that develop over time, in a sequence, or in episodes. Such episodic organizers are described in the next chapter.

Chapter 9

Episodic Organizers

There are two major ways of organizing discourse. Previous chapters focused on superordinate and subordinate relationships—main points and their related ideas; here, the emphasis is on the second major way of organizing discourse: sequence. Sequence is most evident in the unfolding of a story, in the chronological events of history, and in the steps of a scientific process. Episodic organizers depend on students having had numerous experiences with concept organizers (Chapter 8); hence, work with episodic organizers should not begin until the pupils can handle concept organizers with ease. The episodic organizers discussed in this chapter are useful in many content area situations.

VALUE AND USES

Episodic organizers demonstrate order and relationships over time. They emphasize change expressed as one event leading to another or, in a more abstract way, the development of an argument or an essay. They are particularly useful in content areas when students are attempting to understand cause-effect and problem-solution relationships. Episodic organizers also are helpful as preconstructions and postconstructions in reading narratives because they assist learners in understanding story sequence.

This chapter presents specific examples of episodic organizers in a variety of contexts. The examples lead from rather simple episodic organizers using pictures as a basis for understanding time relationships to more complex organizers as bases for written assignments.

EPISODIC ORGANIZERS WITH ONE PICTURE

The teacher who often asks "why" and "what will happen next" questions is preparing students to think episodically. Real events can be very useful for developing cause and effect, predicting outcomes, and sequential thinking. Pictures can help students think about such relationships but must be selected carefully. A boring picture usually will not invite the kind of thinking desired. Pictures should show an activity that by its very nature asks the questions, "how, why, what next?"

Using a picture such as the one in Figure 9–1 (the nature of the picture should, of course, be related to the children's maturity and interest), the teacher should ask what students see happening. It generally is better to pose the question so that children focus on the activity rather than just the things in the picture. The teacher then asks questions that extend the picture into the past as well as into the future.

For example, how did the man get in the old ship? How did the (treasure?) chest get in the ship? To extend the picture into the future, the teacher can ask: What will the man do? What will he find? If students suggest he will find a treasure, the teacher may ask what he will do with it.

By asking such questions, and encouraging childen to think these time relationships through, the teacher develops five episodes:

1. the placing of the treasure in the old ship
2. the man's finding out about the treasure
3. the breaking through the deck of the ship

Figure 9–1
A Basis for
Episodic
Thinking

4. the man's opening the chest and finding the treasure
5. the man's resolving what to do with the treasure

The use of pictures to develop and extend stories works best with a small group or a whole class. The teacher should accept all ideas. The aim is not to develop a great masterpiece of literature but to open the youngsters' minds to story creation and to develop a schema for narration. Of course, reading to children and telling them stories also aid that process. The development of such schemata leads to the eventual writing of stories.

THE 3-SEQUENCE PICTURE STORY

In some cases, it will be necessary to use three pictures to describe a sequence before using a single one, as in the previous activity. The three-sequence picture may be developed orally as well. Cartoons demonstrate simple sequences of actions that motivate children to want to tell a story. The teacher may use telegraphic language and develop the first episodic organizer using a three-picture cartoon sequence.

This type of organizer is presented best by overhead projector. Each child also may have a duplicate copy of the sequence. The teacher first discusses the overall idea behind the sequence, thus developing the macrostructure of the story. The teacher draws an arrow from one picture to the next indicating the flow of events. Each picture is discussed and students are asked to offer their interpretations. People in the pictures should be given names and actual conversations, and comments on them should be encouraged. The teacher then writes on the transparency and the pupils copy. The three-picture episodic organizer shown in Figure 9–2 demonstrates the activity suitable for second grade and beyond.

In this example, the teacher used the children's language. The quotation marks were introduced to indicate to the pupils that the characters were saying something. The use of real names gave the story a stronger narrative style.

After an organizer has been developed, the students should be encouraged to retell the story using the words as cues. Their language should not be telegraphic; rather, they should be encouraged to generate sentences to the best of their abilities. These same stories also can be used to generate written stories, first modeled by the teacher.

This is a natural time to reintroduce paragraphing. The sentences generated about the first picture can be used to compose the first paragraph, and so on.

CAUSE-EFFECT ORGANIZERS

Pictures can be used to develop stories involving causes and effects. A single picture is used and the learners predict the effect of the activity it presents—what may have caused the activity. In the episodic organizer in Figure 9–3, one picture is used, with the possible effect supplied through the children's imaginations. Such an organizer is suitable for some children in grade three and certainly for intermediate grade pupils.

In this organizer, children were able to predict an outcome: an effect that may evolve naturally from a child's playing with fire. A number of stimulating pictures will be needed for children to produce such organizers. The pictures may be photographs, artwork from books and other sources, or sketches drawn by pupils or the teacher.

Figure 9–2
The 3-Picture
Organizer

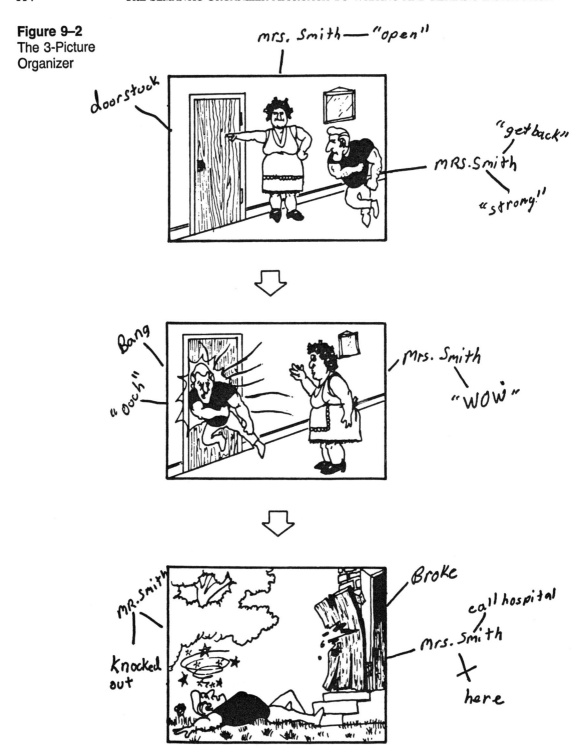

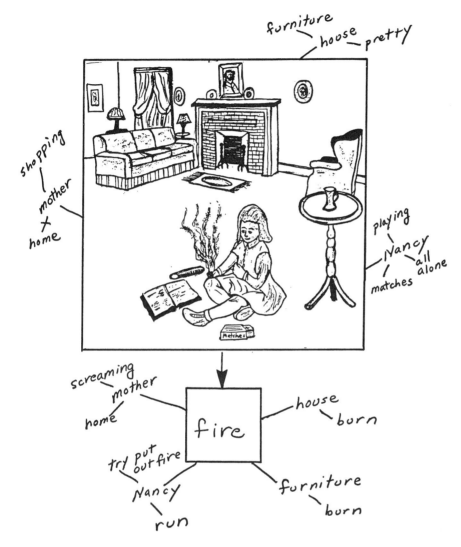

Figure 9–3
A Cause-Effect
Episodic
Organizer:
Cause Phase

Children should have practice retelling stories based on these organizers. Repeated review can help, especially when the youngsters realize that they not only need help in the construction of the organizer but that they also will be expected to retell the story using the organizer as a cuing system. The retelling should occur not only after the construction of the organizer but also the next day, again perhaps several days later, and possibly a week or two still later. The teacher also may want to use these organizers for composing paragraphs. In the fire example, pupils would compose two paragraphs—one for the cause, and one for the effect.

In this example, the picture presents a cause. Figure 9–4 presents an effect and the learners are expected to construct an organizer describing its cause.

Figure 9–4
Cause-Effect
Organizer:
Effect Phase

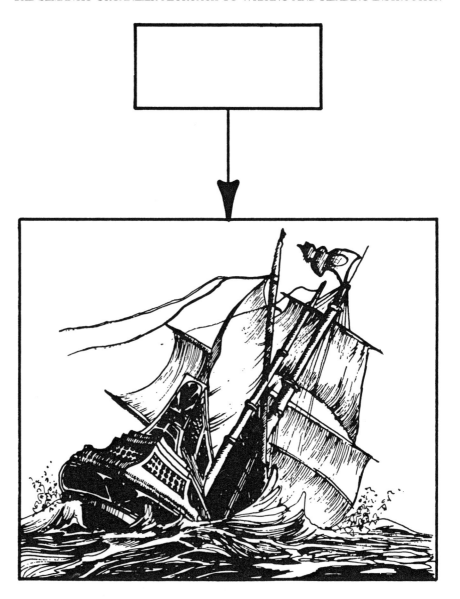

This is likely to be a much more difficult activity for some than the preceding one. It may be necessary for the teacher to role-play activities, to show films, and to point out natural causes for certain events. Again, the children should be expected to retell the story based on the organizer constructed. After practice with retelling, they should be able to write a two-paragraph story based on cause-effect episodic organizers.

Using one picture, intermediate grade pupils and beyond should be instructed next to construct a three-episode organizer. A single picture may be extended into the future and back into the past. For Figure 9–5, the youngsters were required to

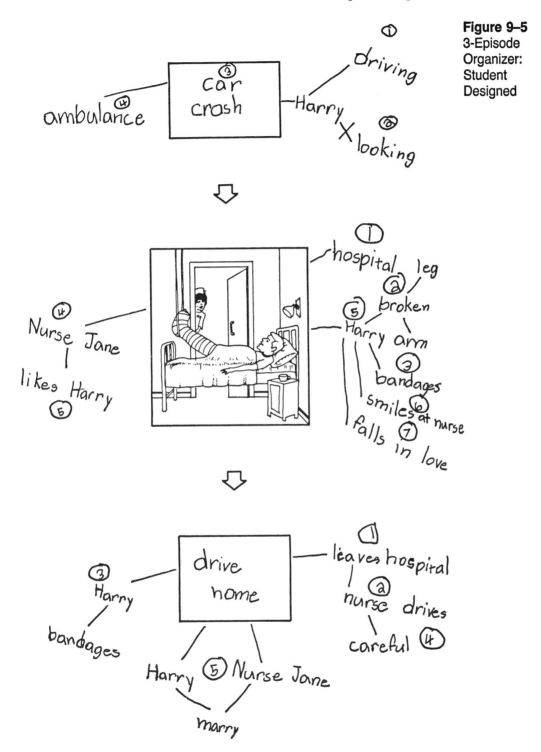

Figure 9–5
3-Episode
Organizer:
Student
Designed

construct the episodic organizer with the teacher modeling the process, then to retell the story. They then composed a three-paragraph story based on the three episodes represented.

This organizer presents not only a sequence from episode to episode but also a sequence within each episode. Numbers on the "legs" of the organizers indicate the sequence within episodes. Children can be introduced to past, present, and future tenses if appropriate to their linguistic development. The class that constructed this organizer composed the following story with some help from the teacher:

> One time Harry was driving his car. He was not looking where he was going. He crashed. The ambulance came and took Harry away.
> Harry is in the hospital. He has a broken leg and a broken arm. He has bandages all over him. Nurse Jane takes care of him. She likes Harry. Harry smiles at Nurse Jane and falls in love.
> Harry will leave the hospital. Nurse Jane will drive. Harry will still have bandages in the car. Nurse Jane will be careful. She will drive home. Nurse Jane and Harry will get married.

Once pupils have been able to demonstrate competence in developing their own episodic organizers by extending a picture into both the future and the past, they may be ready to use a picture as a first of three episodes. They can develop two episodes that follow from the activity in the picture. A more difficult activity, for which some learners may be ready, involves using a picture as the final episode and asking them to develop the first two episodes.

Such episodic picture organizers are helpful for teaching content areas such as history or science. Pictures assist children in describing cause-effect relationships in such content areas. Pictures in old books, in newspapers, and in magazines may be cut out and used for developing such organizers. Once pupils have demonstrated the ability to write three paragraphs from episodic organizers, and after they have had a great deal of practice in doing so, it is time to develop organizers in content areas without the use of pictures.

CONTENT AREA ORGANIZERS

History

Events in history need to be tied together; learning isolated bits of information has little value. It is important that students understand that major events in history usually are related in terms of cause and effect. Although historical events involve relationships among various categories as portrayed in semantic organizers in earlier chapters, the concept of change is essential to understanding history. Episodic organizers take change into account in their patterns.

Episodic organizers are particularly helpful when teaching unit plans. Students may forget events discussed in the beginning of a history unit as the class progresses. Episodic organizers help them retain major topics and understand time relationships as one major event leads to another. For example, a unit on the American Revolution, planned for grade five and above, might involve discussion of many events leading up to it, such as the taxing of the colonies without representation, the Boston Tea Party, the Battle of Bunker Hill, etc. Each event might be dealt with in some depth, then represented in a semantic organizer having American Colonies as its topic. Since these events are important because they led to the Revolution, an episodic organizer can be used to describe this cause-effect relationship.

As illustrated in the episodic organizer (Figure 9–6), it is helpful to draw the first boxes small to represent activities or topics further in the past and increase them in size as events move closer. This helps to show dimensions of time visually. In addition, a time sequence within episodes can be demonstrated in each major part of the organizer: the first event appears at 1 o'clock (upper right side) and sequential events follow clockwise.

This episodic organizer covers an overall series of events. However, each event in turn has its own time sequence and can be represented as an episodic organizer on its own. For example, events that led up to the Boston Tea Party are developed sequentially within their own episodic organizer.

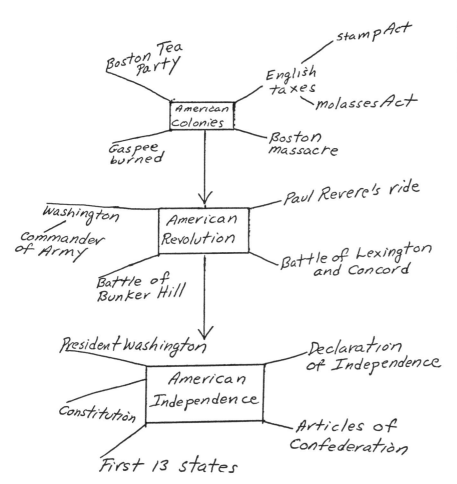

Figure 9–6
Episodic Organizer in a Teaching Unit

Science

The study of science basically involves (1) how things are related to one another and (2) how things change. The first of these can be represented in most cases by noun and concept organizers. How things change are best represented by episodic organizers. For example, the metamorphosis of a monarch butterfly can be described with the episodic organizer in Figure 9–7. This can be developed into four or more paragraphs by students in grade five and above who are able to see the logic of having four paragraphs because there are four episodes.

Figure 9–7
Episodic
Organizer in a
Science Unit

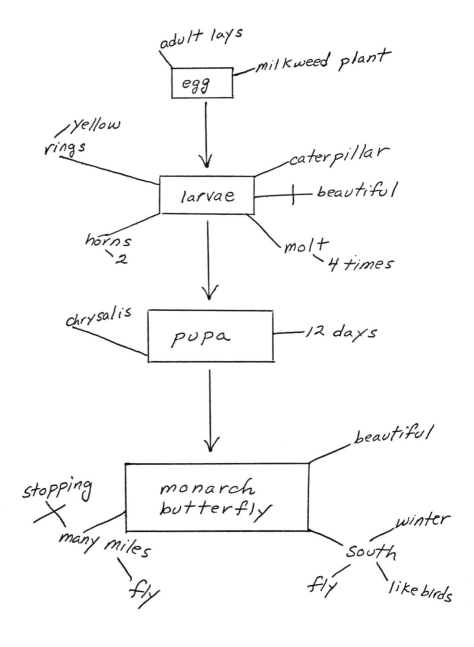

Stories written for children have simple organizational structures—basically, a beginning, a middle, and an end. The rising action takes place at the beginning, the major conflict is in the middle, and the climax and resolution are toward the end. Most of these stories can be formed into a three-episode organizer. Usually each episode is composed of a series of events that can be sequenced in a clockwise series. Figure 9–8 suggests an organization for many simple stories even for primary grade youngsters.

In this figure, each of the three concept organizers provides four steps or events that can be ordered from the 2 o'clock position to the 4 to the 8 and the 10 o'clock. More events or steps could be entered if necessary at appropriate positions. The story of Peter Rabbit (Figure 9–9) follows such a structure.

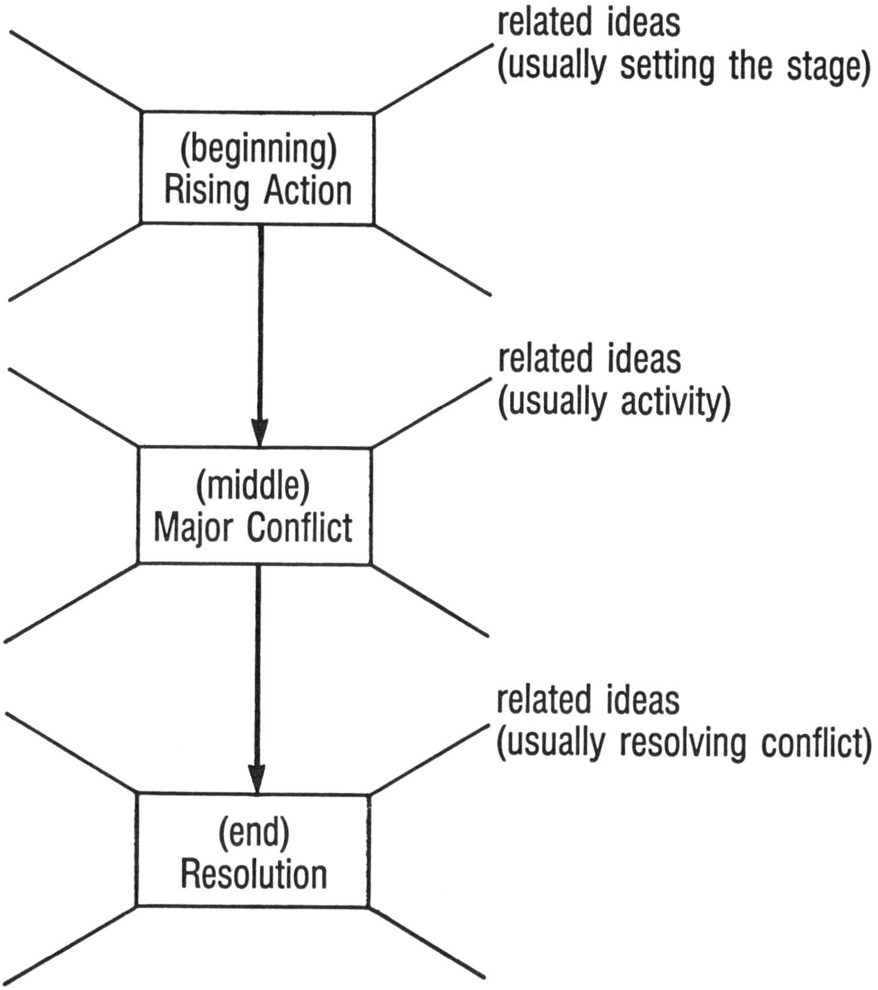

Figure 9–8
Episodic Organizer: Narration

related ideas (usually setting the stage)

(beginning) Rising Action

related ideas (usually activity)

(middle) Major Conflict

related ideas (usually resolving conflict)

(end) Resolution

Figure 9–9
Peter Rabbit
Demonstrates
Narrative Steps

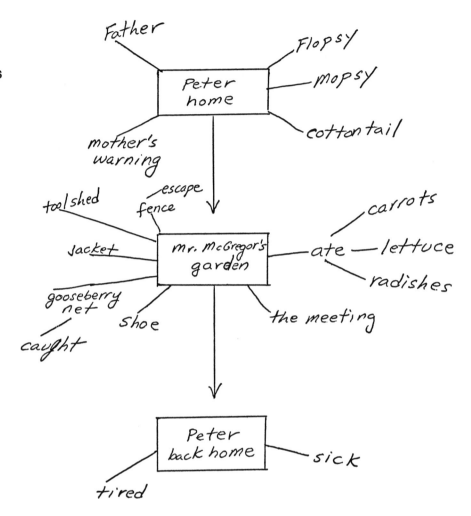

MULTIPLE CAUSES AND EFFECTS

Cause-effect relationships can, of course, be much more complex than those presented earlier. Certainly, two events can occur simultaneously and both together can cause an effect. Similarly, a number of results may stem from a single cause. Episodic organizers are particularly useful in helping students understand and visualize multiple causes and/or effects. Figure 9–10 demonstrates the ways such causes and effects may be diagramed.

The goal of these multiple cause-effect activities is to help pupils note the important relationships. After these relationships are understood at an organized semantic level, the students are better able to concentrate on syntactic issues. When a teacher helps youngsters view relationships in this way before reading, their comprehension during reading usually improves and the distance between reader and

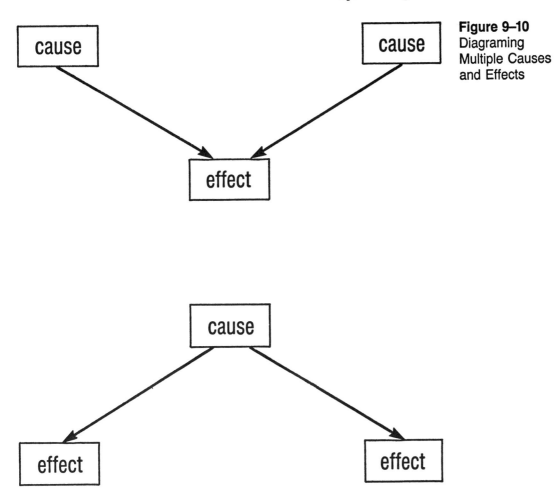

Figure 9–10
Diagraming
Multiple Causes
and Effects

author's intent is minimized. Students are more able to predict resolutions and endings, developing a more mature schema for narratives. Figure 9–11 presents a method for teaching a prediction strategy; pupils are expected to predict the ending by filling in the final concept organizer.

Using this approach, even children in the primary grades can be taught to predict endings; they then read the ending to confirm, reject, or refine their anticipations. They learn to compare their endings with the author's. They also can be introduced to creative narrative writing by rewriting endings of stories to their own liking.

The teacher might begin a story with the class, then ask each youngster to finish it individually. Experience stories, based on actual experiences, also fit into this type of organization. The preparation for a trip fits into the first episode, the trip itself into the second, and the arrival back (with related activities) into the third. The pupils should be expected to write the story or experience in three paragraphs.

Figure 9–11
Cause and
Effect: A
Predictive
Strategy

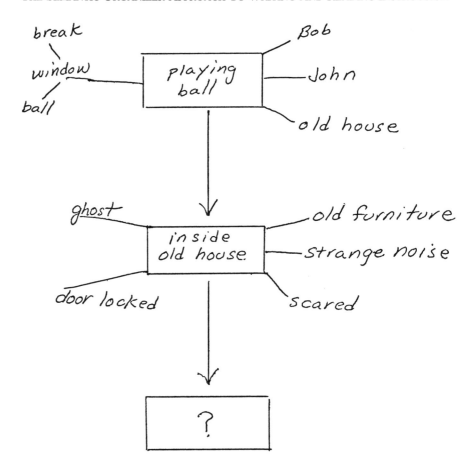

**PROBLEM
AND
SOLUTION**

One practical use of the episodic organizer is to teach pupils to identify specifics of a particular problem, then to show them how to involve those same specifics to suggest one or more solutions. The episodic organizer used for problem solution is a bit more abstract than earlier ones. Instead of writing about a sequence of events that happened, the pupils are confronted with a problem and must develop solutions. The problem is stated much like a present episode while the solution is developed much like a future episode. In actually developing the organizer the pupils represent as many aspects of the problem as possible. These same issues appear again in the solutions. The organizer in Figure 9–12 demonstrates an older learning-disabled student's effort to present his problem and his suggested solution. He cleverly turns his solution into another problem.

Based on the following organizer, the student was able to write two paragraphs:

I have a problem. I have no car. I have license but I soon forget how to drive. I have friends but I don't visit because they live very far. I take

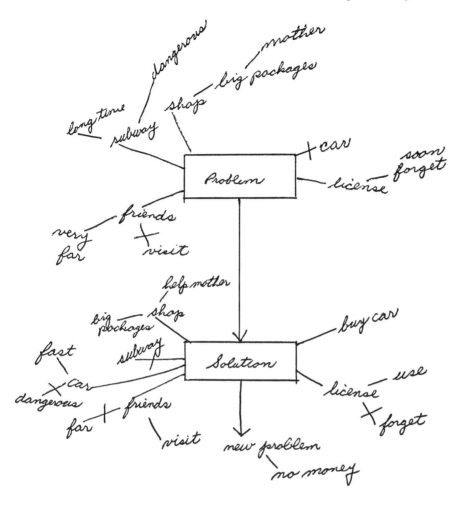

Figure 9–12
Problem
Solving: A
Student's
Difficulties

subway but it takes a long time and dangerous. I shop but sometimes packages too big. My mother carry very big packages.

I have a solution. I can buy a car. I can use my license and I don't forget how to drive. I can visit friends easy and not far by car. I don't take subway. Car is fast and not dangerous. I can have big packages in car and help mother carry big packages. I think it very good idea to buy a car. But I have different problem now. I have no money.

This student usually had great difficulty in writing more than a short paragraph. However, by using such an organizer he was able to write substantially more in a reasonably organized manner. One of the factors that helps the writing is that the ideas and some of the major vocabulary words are represented twice, once in the problem and once in the solution.

TIME-DIMENSION ORGANIZERS

People often use terms referring to the past with no real degree of dimensions in time. For example, past tense can refer to yesterday, two years ago, or centuries ago. Students often appear to have a vague notion of the past as if the concept of "before" had no varying degrees. Teachers use ordinary time lines to provide pupils with a means of understanding the sequence of historical events. Time lines, however, lack a visual dimension for helping students understand various stages in a time sequence.

A time-dimension organizer provides depth visually as a clue to depth in time—past, present, or future. A visual array for teaching time relationships is a tool adaptable for describing a specific series of events or for keying students into recognizing words that clue a time sequence. Although the time-dimension organizer discussed here (Figure 9–13) illustrates both past and future relationships, a teacher may want to use only half or less of the organizer for specific purposes. For example, the left half may be used alone to demonstrate past events while the right half applies only to future events. In either case, the larger box in the middle should be used to represent the present.

This organizer has been developed to demonstrate words that are clues to a time sequence. These words may be helpful for reading and they certainly are helpful for students who need to demonstrate time relationships when writing.

Based on Figure 9–14, Peter, a fifth grader, was able to use the time-related words and to write a short passage with appropriate verb tenses. He constructed his own time-dimension organizer, individualizing a basic design that had been prepared by his resource room teacher. Peter demonstrated the various dimensions of a time sequence in a three-paragraph composition that evolved from his time-dimension organizer:

> Millions of years ago dinosaurs lived. In prehistoric times the earth go. very cold. Dinosaurs ate leaves from trees. When the earth got very cold the trees died. The dinosaurs died because the trees died.
>
> Now dinosaurs don't live. They are all dead and extinct. Sometimes people find dinosaurs bones. Now other animals die and there is a problem.
>
> In the future many animals will die and will be extinct. Many years from now people will find these bones just like the dinosaurs' bones. Maybe people will be extinct millions of years from now.

As students read texts, they should be encouraged to chart their own time-dimension organizers. They can become sensitive to time-related words, which they can add to a class chart. A large time–dimension organizer posted on a bulletin board is helpful when a class or group is involved with a unit that stresses sequential time relationships.

INDEPENDENT ORGANIZING

Once students have mastered concept and episodic organizing with the guidance of the teacher, and have had a multitude of writing and reading experiences, they are usually ready to undertake brainstorming and organizing on their own. Most children who have become used to semantic organizing find it a valuable tool for themselves when they want to write or when they are asked to undertake an instructional reading

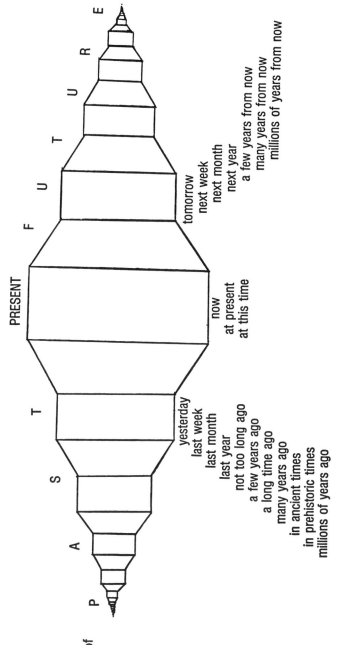

Figure 9-13
Time-
Dimension
Organizer
Clues
Sequences of
Events

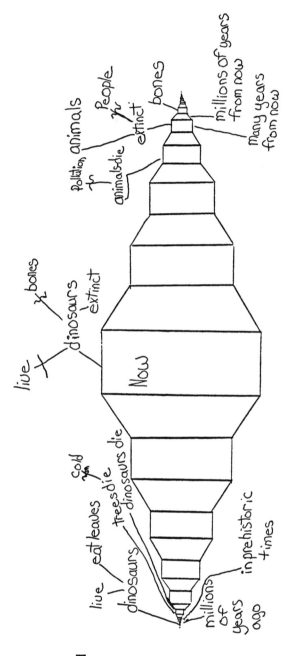

Figure 9–14
A Time-
Dimension
Organizer
Implemented

task. In an elementary school district, where one of the authors of this book served as a consultant, he could hardly walk down a corridor without a child emerging from a classroom to show her or his semantic organizer.

A number of pupils enjoy collaborative organizing. If the teacher will assist pupils in learning how to collaborate (helping each other, not criticizing each other), there is much benefit for youngsters in brainstorming and formulating organizers in preparing for an assigned reading, in laying out the groundwork for a research report, in studying for a unit test, and in just having fun planning a piece of creative writing. (For some specific ideas on helping students become collaborative learners, see Chapter 11, under the heading, Peer Conferencing Model.)

In this chapter, sequences were emphasized and episodic organizers were intro-
CONCLUSION
duced as useful tools for expressing sequence and relationships over a period of time that change as one event leads to another. Episodic organizers provide pupils with important strategies for writing and reading materials arranged in some type of order.

Once students have control over episodic and other types of organizers, they will tend to use them independently or in collaboration with their peers. It is, of course, not necessary for children to formulate organizers when they are aching to read a story for their own enjoyment, or to write a creative story when ideas are pouring out well before a pencil is touched to paper. In the next chapter some ideas are suggested for spontaneous creative writing.

Chapter 10

Spontaneous Creative Writing

External organizers tend to encourage convergent thinking and sequencing—important abilities for many school and life tasks. On the other hand, learners should be assisted in developing divergent and creative thinking abilities spontaneously. Spontaneous writing can be among the most important and memorable experiences students have in school. The best time to help some youngsters become spontaneous writers is after they have had a number of experiences with developing logically sequenced, well-organized compositions based on organizers. By the time they have written successfully with organizers, they should be able to internalize organizational patterns as aids in their spontaneous writing.

Teachers can observe students' readiness to make the transition from organizers to spontaneous writing when they observe that the youngsters' organizers differ in content rather extensively from the substance of the story that is finally produced. For example, in Figure 10–1, Gina, a second grader, was asked to talk about her five senses in relation to popcorn that the teacher was making for the class. Gina organized her senses but developed an imaginative story quite different from the external organizer. Her story was more creative and obviously took a direction more divergent than would be predicted from the rather convergent organizer.

There are many ways to develop and encourage "taking off on your own." The extension of episodic organizers is one natural way to encourage youngsters to create their own stories. Extending episodic organizers is accomplished by providing students with a picture and requesting that they write a story by expanding the activities shown into the past and perhaps into the future.

DEVELOPING SPON-TANEITY

Figure 10–1
From Mundane Organizer to Imaginative Story

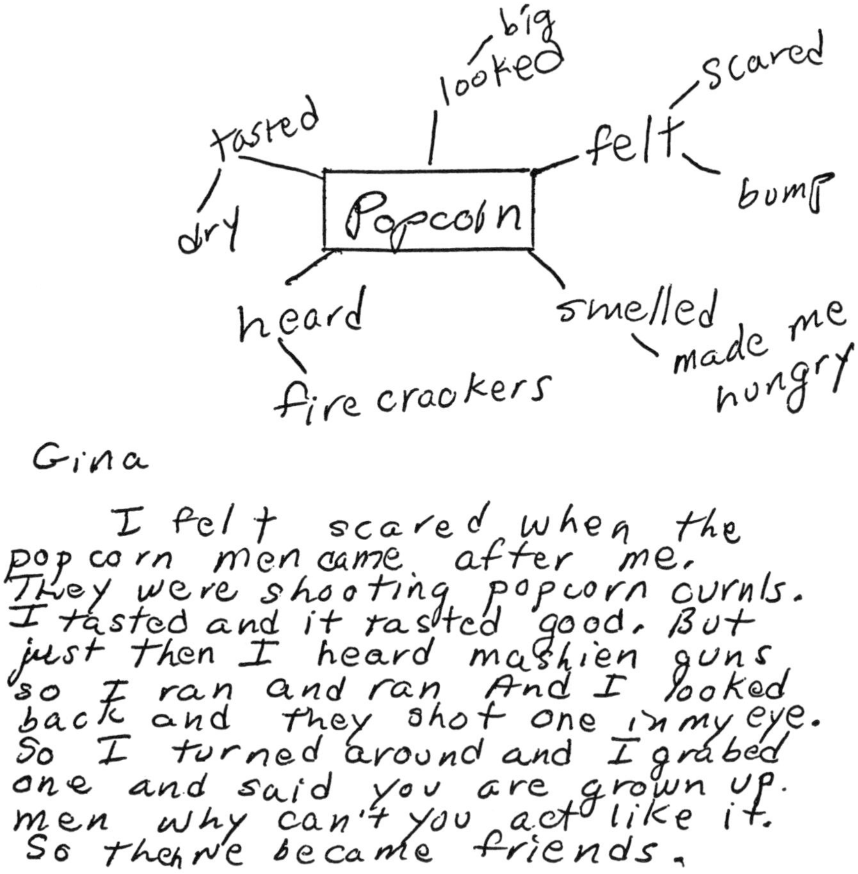
big
looked
scared
tasted
felt
bump
dry
Popcorn
heard
smelled
made me hungry
fire crackers
Gina
I felt scared when the
popcorn men came after me.
They were shooting popcorn curnls.
I tasted and it tasted good. But
just then I heard mashien guns
so I ran and ran And I looked
back and they shot one in my eye.
So I turned around and I grabed
one and said you are grown up.
men why can't you act like it.
So then we became friends.

SOURCES FOR STORY CONTENT

Story content most often is based on students' experiences. However, children have two overall types of experiences. One type is the actual experiences they have when they interact with their environment; these are important and form the thought and language base upon which they can build. However, there is another type that is not capitalized on enough and that, in fact, may be more real for youngsters. This experience involves children's fantasy lives.

Many youngsters who seem to do poorly in school because they are not attending to their lessons seem to have quite active imaginations. Certainly, daydreams are not passive activities; they are very active mental processes. Teachers can tap the energies of these daydreams and fantasies and incorporate them into exciting learning experiences. Numerous pupils build excellent writing and reading strategies when these fantasy experiences are put to creative use. Children need preparation for expanding their imaginations but they also need an encouraging, accepting attitude from the teacher. They need verification that it is quite acceptable to produce creative, imaginative stories in a classroom.

The best way of helping children develop stories based on fantasy is by modeling the process with the class. Once youngsters understand the process, the teacher can work with smaller groups and encourage them to become more independent, resulting in the writing of their own stories. The primary attitude of the teacher must be acceptance: the teacher should be ready and willing to accept what the youngsters offer in developing the story.

One of the blocks to this process is rejection, when youngsters interpret the teacher's attitude as seeming not to approve of some of their ideas. The teacher should not expect great literature from this process. Especially in the beginning, quantity of production is the major aim—quality will follow.

The approach begins with a kind of brainstorming process guided by the teacher; however, no ideas should be edited, as that inhibits production and creative thinking. The teacher should be enthusiastic about what the children offer. This attitude of valuing their ideas is important for motivating the youngsters to continue to produce ideas and language as well as to feel a sense of ownership of their work.

Another important aspect of motivation involves pacing. It is essential that the pace of this writing activity be quick, that the teacher who is doing the writing in the beginning do so spontaneously without worrying about editing. Editing comes later, after the original story is written.

The story process should start with action. Children usually become more interested if the story opens with action rather than with a description of setting. For example, intermediate grade youngsters might be interested in starting a story about a racing car going at 150 miles an hour, or primary grade children might be interested in one that begins with a boy and a girl walking into an old house where someone has said monsters may live.

The teacher should ask the children what they are interested in, what kinds of stories they like to hear, to daydream about, or to watch on television. If there are differences of opinion, the teacher can integrate the ideas. For example, if some youngsters want to write about sports and others about a haunted house, the teacher can combine those ideas and suggest one about boys and girls who were playing a game when the ball went into a haunted house (as in Figure 9–11 in Chapter 9).

It is not necessary that the children have a complete story in mind when they start writing; they merely need some tentative direction as to where it is going. It also is not important that the story be completed in one lesson. Indeed, children's interest can grow from day to day if the teacher presents episodes rather than a complete story.

In a story with parts, after each part is written, the teacher should make copies with a ditto master, carbon paper, or photocopy machine so the youngsters can have a copy. This also is important because the children will be taping the story and will read their parts of it to the recorder. They also will need to know when to make appropriate sound effects for their parts; many primary grade youngsters can learn to make notes or underline their parts so they will be ready for sound effects or for reading their individual parts.

For first or second graders, a single episode usually is sufficient for a whole story; for older youngsters, or those who have sufficient ideas and imagination and who can interrelate longer sequences, it is advisable to compose two to four episodes. Other

STORIES BASED ON FANTASIES

children in the school may wish to read these stories and episodes after they have been edited. They can be advertised by the school librarian in cooperation with the classroom teacher. Those who wrote stories or episodes may wish to construct posters—like movie ads—to spark the interest of prospective readers in their own class and in other classes throughout the school. Children will wait anxiously for the next exciting, thrilling, chilling episode when one episode at a time is featured in the classroom or school library.

AUDIO TAPING

Audio taping helps develop all participants' ability to visualize. In taping stories, the teacher assigns oral reading and sound effects to the pupils. Most of them can (and should) have some role to play, even just as a producer of sound effects. Before taping, oral reading should be practiced and the children should be aware that certain sound effects are needed at specific times. Pupils need to listen carefully and visualize the episode in order to know when to produce appropriate effects.

For example, in a story about a storm at sea, selected children had to listen to others reading in order to make the proper sound effects at the correct times. A piece of clear acetate (used for overhead projectors) was used to simulate the sound of thunder—when thunder was needed, the youngsters rattled the acetate.

Pupils who are going to read parts of the story should practice, underline the part they will present, and be ready at the right time. They need to listen to others and to visualize. More than one child can be used at a time, such as in a crowd scene, when they provide vocal effects. After youngsters have practiced their parts, whether reading individually, reacting with a group, or making sound effects, they should be ready to tape the story.

A high-quality tape recorder with a microphone on a long cord (rather than a built-in microphone) is needed for such group activities. The teacher and the youngsters form a circle around the recorder and the teacher can direct the microphone as the children participate. It also is important that the teacher be accepting of youngsters' reading. Under these conditions, children often will not read exactly what is on the paper, yet their performance—part reading and part ad libbing—will contribute to the recording. Once the story has been taped, the children normally enjoy listening to its being played back. It is particularly fun when exciting episodes end with the words "to be continued."

As part of this taping, background music is beneficial. Classical music can be brought into the classroom this way. For example, some works of Wagner and Beethoven provide excellent background for introducing ghost stories and other adventure stories. When the episode is finished, a short piece of the music can be played while the youngsters are saying, "to be continued." The music and sound effects add interest and fun and provide a professional touch.

When the first episode has been written and taped, it is time to start thinking of the second episode (and subsequent ones). The teacher should allow children to work in groups and to develop their own subsequent episode. The youngsters can share this with one another for enjoyment, then tape it. More than one story can evolve out of the same beginning episode. The teacher may need to work directly with some groups, while others can progress more independently. Often students become so involved with this exciting way of integrating reading, writing, listening, and speaking that they develop sequels to their stories. When this happens, they have learned to visualize.

The stories may be edited by the pupils with the teacher's help, then written into small books. The books can be placed in the classroom library and copies of the tape can be placed in or with each book. Other pupils in the school generally enjoy listening to and reading these stories.

FOLLOW-UP ACTIVITIES

It is useful for youngsters to understand how professional stories are written and published. The teacher may take the children to a book publishing company or to a newspaper plant. Sometimes it is possible to arrange to have authors visit a school or take part in a telephone conference. The teacher, often with the assistance of the librarian, can teach pupils to bind books they have written and the bound books can become permanent additions to a classroom library or even to the school library. The authors' names and the titles of the books can be placed in the library card catalog, just as with any other book.

Of course, when materials are to be "published" as books, they need to be edited carefully. Students should receive help in this process. When stories are not going to be "published" or used for any audience other than immediate peers, the teacher should use the process of selective editing and language expansion discussed in the next chapter.

This chapter focused on ways of helping children organize their ideas without the use of externally developed semantic organizers. Writing should be fun and story writing should be full of surprises for the writer as well as the reader. During the course of writing the writer may find himself or herself moving away from any preconceived plan. The work with semantic organizers that preceded this chapter was meant to assist young writers internalize organizational strategies that will be of use to them as they develop into exciting story writers.

CONCLUSION

Chapter 11

Selective Editing and Language Expansion

Every teacher who must "correct" the reading and written work of students faces problems. This chapter discusses some of the particular difficulties, then offers specific suggestions, based on assessment and performance objectives, for turning correction into selective editing and language expansion.

What to correct, how to correct, and when to correct plague teachers because overcorrection can destroy a student-teacher relationship and result in children's developing a dislike for reading and/or writing. When a teacher corrects all or most of the mistakes on a child's paper, it is highly predictable that the next assignment will result in less production. Similarly, a reader who is corrected for each miscue while reading orally eventually will do anything possible to avoid the activity—even feigning illness.

CAVEATS IN CORRECTING

An unsatisfactory alternative to overcorrection is random correction. Here the teacher, conscious of not filling the page with red marks or stopping the reader too often, points out a variety of mistakes or miscues in a hit-or-miss fashion. This type of correction also frustrates learners for it fails to provide them with the consistency of feedback needed to test out language rules. They are, unconsciously, searching for a pattern that will help them in novel situations.

Another unsatisfactory approach to correcting is placing too much attention on developing less important skills while the student needs to concentrate on one important area. Such correction misguides the learner. For example, Donald's teacher corrected his paper consistently for misspellings while his major need, which was neglected, involved organizing ideas into categories. His teacher misguided Donald, a fifth grader, by directing too much attention to individual words when his greatest need was in the area of his content organization. In misguiding corrections,

137

teachers direct students' attention to inappropriate aspects of language in relation to their major difficulties. Problems related to major needs ought to be resolved at least partially before relatively less important ones are tackled.

SELECTIVE EDITING

While adults permit and encourage trial and error in oral development by attending to the meaning of the children's language, they tend to change the emphasis when dealing with written language. However, and unfortunately, neither trial nor, most of all, error is considered a legitimate strategy for written language development by a number of teachers. While it probably is true that a more direct approach is necessary in guiding children to expand and correct their written than their oral language, teachers' sensitivity to how they correct is essential. Editing and guiding seem more useful than correction.

Teachers can help children edit their writing and can give direction to the youngsters' reading. In editing writing and in directing reading, the meaning and efficiency of communication must be emphasized.

The Value of Mistakes

The success of editing and directing depends first of all on an attitude that mistakes are important for the learning process because trial and error are basic to learning. Children learn by trial and error long before they come to school. It is amazing how much they learn through this process. By falling, they learn to walk; by mispronouncing, they learn to speak; by hurting themselves, they learn to be careful; by trying to read and write and noting that some messages do and some do not make sense, they learn to become readers and writers. Teachers can help students verify their right to trial and error, a process that they bring to school but that too often is ignored and even rejected.

A child's mistakes also are important for the teacher, who otherwise will not know how to help or where help is needed. Mistakes can be cues to the learner's strategy and skills. Mistakes are extremely helpful for proper assessment and for the setting of objectives.

Assessment

For both writing and reading, it is essential that the teacher and/or parent and child know the specific objectives for editing and writing and guiding the reading. Objectives must be developed based on an assessment. Informal assessment (monitoring) probably is the most valid type for developing objectives; monitoring thus is based on normal reading and writing activities in a natural setting. Children should feel relaxed and not threatened. A test-like atmosphere is inappropriate; the assessment should take place in a normal every-day type of environment. A child who is tense will fail to demonstrate true abilities in both reading and writing. A certain quantity of production is essential for it is important to assess and develop objectives based on patterns. Few patterns emerge without considerable production.

Sufficient quantity of production also is essential for continuing assessment, since that takes place not only at the beginning of a program but throughout it. Every writing and reading activity must be assessed in relation to the objectives set by the child in collaboration with the teacher. When pupils achieve objectives to a satisfactory level, it is time for teacher and pupil to set new ones based on the pattern that has been observed during many writing and reading activities. Once new goals have been set, youngsters should continue to be held responsible for previous objectives, although sometimes the earlier ones may receive less attention from the children and may suffer slightly. Reminders, devoid of negative comments, will help. Since assessment must be based on quantity of production, it is critical that the teacher's attitude be positive. Quality will not develop if the pupils do not produce or if they are too tense to demonstrate true abilities.

In assessing writing and reading, teachers should ask questions in a particular sequence:

1. Has the child produced enough for a valuable and reliable assessment?
2. Does the child's writing or reading make sense?
3. Does the child communicate meaning efficiently?
4. Does the reader or listener need to struggle to understand what the child has read or written?

Such questions deal with quantity, meaning, and efficiency. If there are needs in any of these areas, more specific questions must be asked:

1. Why is the child failing to produce?
2. Is the writing well organized?
3. Do sentence structures create problems?
4. Are words used appropriately?
5. Are words spelled correctly?
6. Is there a problem with the child's understanding of the overall or immediate context if the oral reading does not make sense to the listener?
7. Is the problem related only to the child's not knowing or not recognizing a word?

As patterns of errors or miscues become apparent, the teacher should establish objectives based on the questions, then practice selective editing and/or direction. Selective editing means that not every mistake on a paper will be corrected. Many will be left for future objectives. The teacher should develop perhaps one, two, or three objectives for a child and edit only errors or miscues related to those points.

Sometimes parents show concern when a child returns home with a writing assignment that has only been "partially corrected" by a teacher. To avoid conflict and misunderstanding, the teacher needs to inform the parents why this is done, including stating writing and reading objectives clearly on a form sent to the home. In addition, a stamp at the top of each page can be used to identify for the child, parents, and even the teacher the objectives in the selective editing. This stamp should read: "This paper has been edited for —————," with the objectives filled in by the teacher.

Through the use of such a stamp, the teacher continually focuses on editing for objectives and is less likely to get off the track by overcorrecting, randomly correcting, or misguiding correction. Parents generally are satisfied with this approach and are less concerned that the teacher is not correcting every mistake on the page. More importantly, however, this stamp helps students to focus on objectives; if the goals are appropriate, the pupils will accomplish them satisfactorily. This feeling of successful accomplishment can be one of the major motivators for continuing to produce and to mature in written language development.

Selective Guidance in Reading

There are legitimate purposes for oral reading, such as communicating ideas and entertaining others. However, having a child read publicly in order to correct mistakes is not a legitimate purpose for oral reading. It is bad enough when a teacher corrects every mistake, but in some classrooms other children compete for the chance to correct a reader. When a pupil reads aloud, classmates should not be following the text in order to catch mistakes; instead, they should be listening, gaining information, being entertained by the oral reading.

The child who is reading should have had an opportunity to prepare the selection. The teacher should guide the pupil in concentrating on making sense out of what is being read. If many word recognition errors occur that interfere with understanding the meaning, the youngster should not be encouraged to continue reading. As long as the child is making sense and not changing the author's meaning significantly, neither the teacher nor the classmates should interrupt. The teacher may do so, however, to inform the youngster that what was just read did not make sense. During oral reading, the teacher may simply listen or may read along silently and jot down word recognition errors to be addressed in later lessons.

Through this process, children soon learn that the purpose of oral reading is to inform or to entertain others. They learn that they must prepare the material before reading to others. One way of preparing children for reading orally is to have them listen to a tape recording (perhaps by the teacher) of the passage they are preparing. They thus can prepare the passage by repeated listening and by following the tape as they read silently.

In this way many youngsters who otherwise would fail at oral reading will be successful and will be motivated to read more. With such preparation many children who frustrate themselves during oral reading and develop a negative attitude toward reading in general find themselves successful. They generally are able to make sense out of what they read. Frequently, other children can help youngsters prepare their oral reading. Peer conferencing (discussed later in this chapter) is valuable as long as youngsters realize that they must listen for the meaning and interrupt only if the oral reading makes no sense.

Oral reading and writing can be combined into a valuable activity. For example, Thomas wrote an exciting story about a haunted house. With the teacher's help the paper was edited for logical organization. Thomas rewrote his story, then read it to a small peer group. Those children enjoyed listening to his story and encouraged him to read it to the entire class. The class did listen, then encouraged Thomas to edit the entire story. With the teacher's help, his story was fully edited and a copy was placed in the school library. Thomas, who had been reluctant to write or to read, soon became a prolific writer and improved in both.

In defining objectives, the teacher should consider which processes are most appropriate to focus on at that time for that particular learner. The teacher can be guided by the four main questions, and the subsequent subquestions, in the section on Assessment earlier in this chapter. After ascertaining that enough has been written to assess, the teacher and student should concentrate on, "Does it make sense?" If there are problems in the sense of the presentation, the teacher should formulate a plan concentrating on helping the youngster to think through what to say in logical and/or sequential fashion. Other errors should be disregarded until that question can be answered affirmatively.

When youngsters have difficulty with paragraph structure, it may be linked to a lack of organization in the initial brainstorming process. Students should be guided back to verb, noun, or concept organizers.

Some young pupils think through what they want to write and present the ideas logically but need help in editing for sentence boundaries. For example, Brad, a 7-year-old, responded to a teacher's question about "what he did yesterday" by writing:

> Yesterday mommy look at my room with dirt all the time mommy clean toys on floor clothes in bed mommy gets angry clean up room don't play outside all day

A semantic organizer helped Brad understand sentence boundaries. Each arm of a noun organizer was developed into a sentence. (See Figure 11–1.)

Selective Editing of Writing

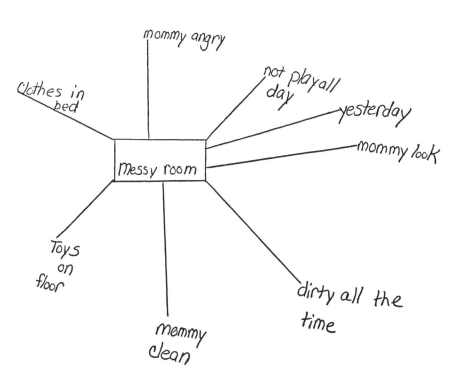

Figure 11–1
Noun Organizer as a Guide to Sentences

Brad produced the following paragraph based on the semantic organizer he developed with the teacher in editing his earlier work. It often is helpful to begin with the topic, in this case "yesterday," at the 1 o'clock position and proceed around clockwise.

Yesterday my room was messy. Mommy looked at my room. My room is dirty all the time. Mommy cleaned my room. Toys were on the floor. Clothes were on the bed. Mommy was angry. I did not play outside all day.

Brad's story still needs work if it is to convey meaning to a larger audience but he has come a long way from his original draft.

The editing of written work with nonstandard constructions must be approached carefully and with understanding. Students often have a pattern to their nonstandard constructions. For instance, in the paragraph below, Carl, who had severe problems with language expression, demonstrated his own mental rule system. The paragraph was written in response to a picture of a barroom brawl in a Western movie.

The man was shoot to the man. The cowboy hit to the man. The chair break. The man run to the door. He blood to the shirt.

Although Carl diverges from standard English in several ways, one obvious pattern shows the use of a nonstandard rule: After a verb, the preposition "to" usually is used. Carl seemed to have developed his own rule: The word "to" follows a verb of action. This rule apparently does not apply after a process verb (break), or perhaps when the verb ends the sentence.

Learners who develop nonstandard rules of syntax need practice with the standard constructions so they can internalize a new set of rules. Carl needs to learn to edit his own writing.

The teacher can accept the logic of the deviant rule because, in this example, there is logic in using "to" after each of the verbs because there is motion forward—forward "to" something. Carl appears to have overgeneralized a standard rule: After some verbs of action such as "run," it is appropriate to use the preposition "to." The teacher set up many situations in which Carl had to use similar constructions. The central focus in these assignments involved the accommodation of a schema, a change in Carl's deviant rule to a standard grammatical rule.

The episodic organizer in Figure 11–2 demonstrates how a deviant rule such as Carl's can be changed while still working within a context larger than a single sentence. This semantic organizer emphasizes the verb "ran to." Rather than getting involved with a prepositional phrase, "to the house," the teacher taught "ran to" as a "verb" and "the house" as the direct object of the verb. In the episodic organizer Carl had to select the appropriate "verb" (in this case "ran to"), complete the semantic organizer, and write a short story. (Note that Carl's reasoning is different from the more common version—the fireman running toward the house. Carl felt that the fireman was the wisest of all.)

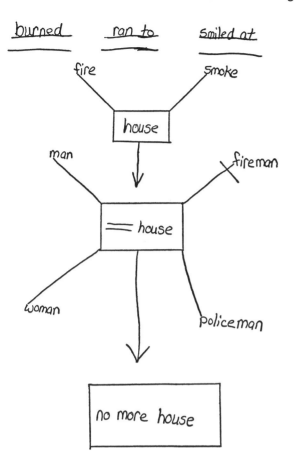

Figure 11–2
Bringing a
Deviant Rule
under Control

Smoke came from a house. The house was on fire.

A man ran to the house. A woman ran to the house. A policeman ran to the house. But the fireman did not run to the house

There was no more house.

This example emphasizes the "verb" "ran to" but avoids sentence drill. By emphasizing a particular linguistic structure within a context, there is a much greater chance that the learning of the new rule and the accommodating of the old can be generalized to other situations.

EXPANDING LANGUAGE

The editing process need not focus totally on miscues or mistakes. Objectives should focus also on expanding what is correct already. The teacher can respond to a student's ideas by writing comments on the side or bottom of the paper and indicate that the message is being understood. The teacher also can encourage additional related writing. For example, when Henry wrote about his adventure in an abandoned house, the teacher wrote the following comments on the paper: "I'm glad you didn't get hurt." "That sounds very frightening." "I bet you were a little scared when that happened." Henry took time to respond to these comments and wrote a short note explaining that he wasn't scared at all because he was brave. Such interaction is what writing is all about.

In addition to responding to the meaning, the teacher may want to point out other positive aspects of the writing. For example, Henry's teacher circled one sentence and wrote, "I like the way you wrote this." Another sentence was circled with the comment simply, "Good idea."

The encouragement of language expansion also may be focused on syntactic structures. For example, some students appear too comfortable using grammatical but very simple sentences. They often produce rather stilted language structures with repetitive sentence patterns. They need to be encouraged to take greater risks and to experiment with language. Semantic organizers can be used to demonstrate to pupils that while basic relationships can remain the same, the syntactic structures can become more complex and more efficient. Students should be encouraged to experiment with style and complexity.

One of the most difficult linguistic constructions for many children is understanding the relation between a pronoun or other part of speech (anaphora) and its referent. Some types of such anaphoric relationships confuse even mature readers. One of the paradoxes of this problem is that words such as "it," "he," "she" are considered "easy" words by many authors of children's reading programs. These words also are considered "easy" in readability formulas.

The word "it" can refer to anything at all. "It" can refer to complex and abstract ideas. "It" can refer to Einstein's Theory of Relativity; hence, "it" can be vastly difficult to understand when its referent is difficult to determine. However, that is only part of the problem. The real problem is trying to teach a student to ascertain where the referent is within a passage. At times the referent is in the same sentence, at other times elsewhere in the paragraph, and at still other times not even in the same paragraph. The pronoun "it" can even change referents within the same paragraph.

Not all of the problems with "it" can be solved here. However, a procedure for beginning to teach pronouns is offered. An initial concern in teaching pronouns is that students must realize there is always a referent that must be discovered. A semantic organizer can help in explaining how to use a pronoun when it is related to a referent that is the topic. In such a procedure, the noun organizer is useful. The topic noun is placed in the box and children are reminded of how to write a paragraph by repeating the same noun over and over. For example:

Dogs run. Dogs bark. Dogs play. (etc.)

Fly

run

Dogs (They)

Play

Bark

Figure 11–3
The Noun
Organizer
Helps Explain
Pronouns

Dogs run. They bark. They play. They don't fly.

They then are shown that the noun does not have to be repeated but that the pronoun "they" can be substituted once the noun has been established (written once). The pronoun "they" should be placed under the noun in the noun organizer. The students then are shown how to write a paragraph using the pronoun. (See Figure 11–3.)

In the next procedure, basic semantic organizers are used to teach that longer sentences can be composed of smaller sentences. This is accomplished at the simplest level by teaching compound subjects and verbs. The teacher can review the basic verb organizer and demonstrate how one sentence can be written instead of two, as in Figure 11–4. These can be expanded rather easily to include more than two nouns.

Noun organizers also can be developed by compounding the verbs (Figure 11–5). A good deal of flexibility of style should be encouraged as pupils combine their understanding of compounds as well as pronouns.

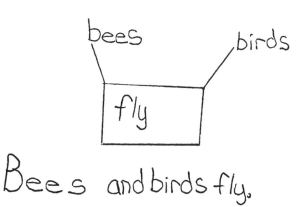

Figure 11–4
Verb Organizer
with Compound
Subject

bees

birds

fly

Bees and birds fly.

Figure 11–5
Noun Organizer
with Compound
Verbs

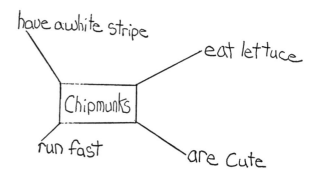

Chipmunks eat lettuce, have a white stripe, run fast, and are cute.

One type of complex sentence that can cause children difficulty in processing deals with cause-effect relationships. Frequently the problem involves the use of the connective "because" as it relates to a sequence of events. For example, many sentences of the following type are formed in written materials with the "because" clause following the main clause:

Harry ate the bread because he was hungry.

In this sentence, Harry's hunger preceded his eating, yet the order of the clauses might indicate that eating preceded hunger. For immature readers and for children who are just starting to write with any kind of complexity, it might be best to begin most of the cause-effect sentences with the subordinate clause, thereby, in this instance, placing the "because" in an initial position.

Because Harry was hungry, he ate the bread.

Events in history that involve cause-effect relationships can be represented by episodic organizers. Pupils are expected to write paragraphs using sentences with "because" clauses, as in Figure 11–6.

One of the major points in this book has been to demonstrate that sentences should not be taught in isolation: The paragraph is the basic unit. This applies to teaching complex sentences. It is far better to develop sentences within the framework of connected text than in isolation.

Another type of complex sentence pupils find early in textbooks is the clause involving relative pronouns such as "who," "which," and "that," or relative adverbs such as "where," "when," "why," and "after." Practice with such complex sentences can be based on noun organizers. One way of providing this practice is through description. Youngsters can be asked to develop a simple noun organizer describing a classmate. Based on the noun organizer, the teacher can demonstrate how individual clauses can be embedded or combined into single

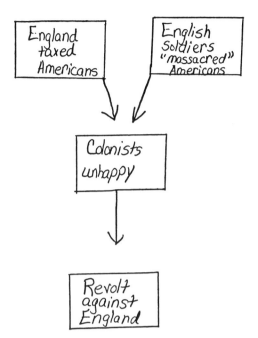

Figure 11–6
Episodic
Organizer Aids
Use of
'Because'
Clauses

Because England taxed Americans, colonists were unhappy. Because English soldiers massacred Americans, colonists were unhappy. Because colonists were unhappy, they revolted against England.

sentences. The teacher draws a circle around the potential clauses to be included in one sentence, as in Figure 11–7.

A student can be aided in developing such complex sentences by a series of steps. First, the child must recognize the relationships as represented by the semantic organizer. Next, the pupil writes two independent sentences:

Johnny has blond hair.
Johnny is very tall.

The subject of the first sentence is changed to "who."

who has blond hair
Johnny is very tall

The second sentence is then inserted into the first and a complex sentence results:

Johnny who has blond hair is very tall.

Figure 11–7
Noun Organizer
and Embedded
Clause

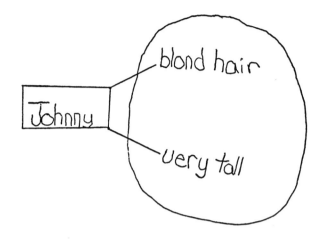

Johnny who has blond hair is very tall.

There is a potential problem with such sentence combining. The approach can become too mechanical unless the relationships are stressed constantly by using semantic organizers.

Based on the semantic organizers described in this and other chapters, a pupil should be able to write a rather well-developed series of paragraphs with a variety of styles. The intermediate grade child should be able to demonstrate paragraph organization, use of pronouns, compound pronouns and verbs, compound sentences, and complex sentences. Figure 11–8 demonstrates how these various linguistic structures and relationships can be developed into two paragraphs representing a rather mature style for a fourth grader who had had many problems expressing himself in written discourse.

**PEER
CONFERENC-
ING**

The teacher has been discussed as the editor in collaboration with the writer. And much of the time the teacher is the significant, knowledgeable adult. It is possible, however, for the teacher to train class members—over time—to assist in the editing.

Training pupils to aid each other in editing their writing takes much time and much practice. Children must learn to respect each other's ideas and to be considerate in helping peers clarify their writing. They must realize that they help others edit their writing in relation to an intended audience. When an audience shares ideas with the writer, many ideas that seem implicit may be understood because experiences are shared. On the other hand, when there is some distance between writer and audience, the text must be as explicit as possible.

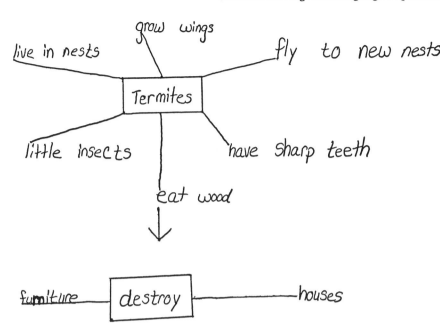

Figure 11–8
Again,
'Ta-dah!'—
Complexity
Begins to
Emerge

Termites which are little insects live in nests. They grow wings and fly to new nests. They have sharp teeth and they eat wood. Because termites eat wood, they destroy furniture. They destroy houses.

Initial emphasis under any conditions should be on clarification of ideas. Peers should be trained to raise such questions as: "What do you mean?" "I don't understand this, could you please explain it?" "Could you give an example?" Peers might ask about the use or spelling of a given word if the message is unclear, but emphasis should be on ideas before mechanics. As students learn to help one another, and with subsequent drafts, many mechanical problems take care of themselves.

Hittleman has developed a clear and useful model of peer conferencing.[1] She suggested the following steps over a minimum of fifteen sessions:

PEER CONFERENCING MODEL

1. Teacher helps pupils prepare a chart with the first column highlighting such occupations as cook, clothes designer, architect, etc. In the second column have children contribute ideas about what these workers do—cooks prepare

food, etc. In a third column have children decide how they receive feedback—cooks ask people to taste food, ask how it is, and what could make it better, etc.

2. Pupils describe personal experiences in which they changed a way they did something based on feedback.

3. Teacher explains that writers depend on feedback to improve their early drafts. Teacher reads his or her own prepared draft of a story and asks for pupils' help in improving it. A copy, prepared for an overhead projector, is then marked up in front of the children—question mark for clarification, the word "more" for additional information, etc.

4. Teacher reads revised draft to class and discusses with pupils those comments and questions that were most helpful for revision. Teacher reads another draft of a story to pupils who once again raise questions and make suggestions as in number 3 above.

5. Pupils who wish to do so write their own stories, and some volunteer to have their drafts placed on the overhead projector the next day. The next day they read their drafts and then show how they make notes on the transparency that will help them revise.

6. Some pupils will show difficulty in focusing questions on main intent or meaning of the draft. Teacher prepares a Peer Response Notes Sheet and models it with another teacher-written draft. On the left side of the sheet pupils summarize the teacher's draft; on the right side they write their comments and questions. Discussion clarifies.

7. All pupils write a draft of a new story in preparation for sharing them with their classmates to practice receiving and giving peer responses.

8. Over about five class sessions, the "fish bowl" technique is used. A small group of pupils sit at the front of the room and each reads his or her own draft aloud to the group while the group and the class listen. After a second reading the peer conference group members summarize the draft and write comments or questions on their Peer Response Notes Sheet. Each member of the group then receives responses and marks her or his draft to indicate the need to clarify, provide additional information, or rearrange. The class observes the process for each day afterward another small group will occupy the "fish bowl" position. Before each subsequent "fish bowl" group meets each day, however, children in the earlier "fish bowl" read their drafts to everyone and discuss when and why they revised or did not revise.

9. Children then prepare another story and work on their own in groups throughout the room as the teacher circulates and acts as facilitator. Children revise their drafts based on the feedback.

10. Throughout the process the teacher and pupils add to two lists of questions and comments—one that has been helpful and one that has not. At this point it is useful to review and revise the list. Example: (1) Helpful Questions and Comments—Ask for more information. Ask for definitions. Clear up confusing ideas. Tell how you felt or acted at a certain part. (2) Non-helpful Questions and Comments—Just saying someone liked it or didn't like it.

Saying it was good or bad or right or wrong. Asking about or criticizing spelling, grammar, etc. Saying what the reader thinks should be said.

11. Pupils should now have another opportunity to go through the whole process of writing a story, meeting in peer conference groups, revising based on peer feedback, and discussing their revision processes. The total process, with teacher guidance when necessary, may need to be practiced over a period of time, dependent upon the class. When the children have become totally familiar with the process and tend to ask useful questions and make helpful comments, they should be ready to function on their own in small groups or teams in their future writing tasks.

Students sometimes help each other in asking for clarification of points in a semantic organizer before the first written draft. However, such peer interaction, at this stage and later, is possible only after a class atmosphere of mutual support has been developed as in the Hittleman model. Such attitudes toward helping one another can be modeled and nurtured by teachers who have a positive approach toward errors, miscues, editing, and language expansion.

CONCLUSION

Selective editing and helping to expand language are means of strengthening reading and writing strategies that should replace general, overall correction of performance. When selective editing is tied to objectives formulated and understood by teacher and pupils, children want to turn to the tasks of improving their performances. They will also, with careful modeling, become aware of how they can help each other.

NOTE

1. Carol G. Hittleman, "Peer Conference Groups and Teacher Written Comments as Influences on Revision During the Composing Process of Fourth Grade Students" (Ed.D. diss., Hofstra University, 1983).

Chapter 12

Emphasis on Thought and Study

In addition to the specific writing/reading functions of the several types of semantic organizers described in earlier chapters, organizers are extremely useful in consciousness building for higher level thinking processes. They also are valuable in promoting more efficient and effective study strategies. This chapter presents ways of making older students (junior high school levels and even beyond) aware of patterns of thinking, of coping with complexities in advanced reading and writing, and of enhancing their abilities to recognize relationships of varied ideas and to retain those ideas.

ORGANIZERS FOR PROMOTING THINKING

Semantic organizers in earlier chapters served as specific aids in developing writing and reading abilities. Although they frequently emphasized patterns of thinking, they were used primarily to cope with a given reading/writing task. This section offers some of the same patterns but the focus here is on building the ability to transfer the thinking pattern from task to task rather than on the task itself. To ensure conscious transfer, students must become aware of the patterns in a variety of reading situations and must have the opportunity to use them in planned writing activities.

Depending on the nature of the material to be written or read, pupils may use concept and/or episodic organizers. As indicated earlier, concept organizers clarify ideas when the material is superordinate/subordinate (major ideas/supporting ideas); episodic organizers are most helpful when those ideas are presented in a sequential or chronological order. Sometimes complex writing will feature just one or the other of these basic patterns; most frequently, however, mature writing is an intermix of superordinate/subordinate and sequence. That is where episodic and concept organizers can be used in conjunction with one another. This chapter examines concept organizers to promote thinking, then episodic organizers, and finally a combination of both.

Concept Organizers

Generalizing

When facts are known but need to be generalized for a given purpose, a basic concept organizer is useful. Too often the "main idea" of a passage is obvious to the teacher but not to the student. Arriving at, or even recognizing, the statement of a main idea involves a rather high-level generalization that must draw on conscious experiences with other types of generalizations. In fact, learners must be able to understand that some type of generalization is being called for when they view the subordinate data if they are to arrive at the superordinate idea.

For example, a passage introduced in a seventh grade social studies class described the activities of a woman who traveled and spoke about education, taxes, health programs, and defense. It was never stated directly that she was campaigning for a political job, but students were expected to generalize the concept. A way of helping them with this generalizing is to build concept organizers focused on problems confronting the class or on school elections when feasible. The laying out of subordinate points around a circle with a question mark in it, and with appropriate teacher guidance, will help them change the question mark to the notion of campaigning. Then a concept organizer can be constructed about the woman's campaigning for election. Students should be helped to internalize this use of a concept organizer—generalizing. In this instance, the passage about campaigning is only a means to an end.

Drawing Conclusions

Another type of generalizing, drawing conclusions, can be helped with concept organizers. For example, an eighth grade student chose to learn more about three creatures that bothered him—mosquitoes, house flies, and spiders. He drew three separate concept organizers and entered the vital information about each around the circle he had drawn with the name of each creature in it. His teacher then asked if he had drawn any one large conclusion about the three. The student drew a blank circle in the middle of a piece of paper and put his three concept organizers around it with a line drawn from each to the blank middle circle. He finally wrote "sophisticated creatures" in the middle circle for, as he analyzed his data, he realized that this was a conclusion he could draw. The resulting diagram was of value to others because they could see readily why he arrived at such a conclusion.

Comparing

Two simple concept organizers can be used in conjunction with one another to express comparison. For example, two philosophies can be compared by drawing two organizers side by side and placing the names of the philosophies in the center of each. Similarities and differences can be described by arranging the similarities in the space between the two organizers, then drawing lines from each circle to the similar idea. Differences can be expressed by writing the key words on the far side of each organizer. Or a ven diagram can be used where differences are written in the outer part of each circle and similarities in the part of each circle that links.

Differences and similarities related to the same topic can be expressed by using three simple concept organizers. For instance, fact and fiction in regard to Count Dracula could be demonstrated first by placing his name in the center of one circle, with two other circles on either side with the word "fact" written in one and "fiction" in the other. Lines are drawn from each of these circles to the circle with his name. Factual and fictional information then are entered in each of the outer circles.

Students frequently find it difficult to recognize, understand, and relate two sides of an argument. Concept organizers can be used to describe opposing points of view in much the same manner as the Count Dracula example. For example, a student chose to demonstrate the pros and cons of gun control. The organizer consists of three circles with the phrase "gun control" in the middle one, "pro" on one outer circle and "con" on the other. Differences are written on the outer side of each circle. Any similarities could be placed between the circles. In this case, the pupil wrote "stop crime" between the circles.

Contrasting

Writing or reading a sequence of ideas often is considered a relatively simple task but it is not always so. For example, in a passage about ghost towns, the present zero population situation was discussed first, followed immediately by the causes. Ideas were given as to why such towns developed originally and how they were built. Since the overall ideas represented a sequence not easily visible in the passage, the construction of an episodic organizer helped the eighth graders involved in the discussion view and understand the sequence of events.

Episodic Organizers

Sequence of Ideas

Students can benefit from reading stories created by others. Sometimes, however, in retelling or reporting on a story, they have difficulty ordering the main events. Some youngsters concentrate too heavily on one episode at the expense of the others. Some don't recognize the episodes. The episodic organizer helps readers structure and demonstrate their understanding of the flow of events.

Story Structure

Learners should construct a three-episode organizer. Major episodes or sets of events can be guided by the teacher as pupils are asked to think first about the most important things that happened in the beginning of the story, then the middle, then the end. For example, even a long story such as *Gone With the Wind* can be organized around three major episodes—before the war, during the war, and after the war. Even the separate characters can be described using an episodic organizer.

As shown in Chapter 9, episodic organizers are particularly useful in expressing cause–effect relationships. One student, for example, expressed the multiple causes for World War I by arranging relatively small circles at the top of a page and placing one large circle with the words "World War I" toward the bottom. The smaller circles were presented in such a way that the earlier causes could be written in those nearer the top and the more immediate causes in those nearer the middle. Lines then were drawn to show how events were related to one another and all were connected to the effect—the war.

Cause-Effect Relationships

Episodic organizers are especially useful in helping learners understand how to predict outcomes. For instance, children in one class were taught to develop the first two parts of a three-episode organizer as they read a story from their basic reader. Next, they stopped reading and developed the third part of the organizer based solely on their expectations of how the story would end. They then resumed reading with high motivation: to learn whether they were right about the ending. The pupils were

Prediction of Outcomes

helped to understand why the author arrived at the given ending but were praised for their creative endings. Many of the endings seemed more logical and/or interesting than that of the author.

Writing Stories

Episodic organizers provide a relatively simple way to get started in planning one's own writing of a story. As noted, almost all stories can be organized in three major episodes: beginning, middle, and end. If the episodic organizer is planned carefully, the resulting writing usually will be well structured and can take the form of a short story or a longer story with three chapters.

Writing Essays

Essay writing can pose a problem for students for they must develop and show the flow of an argument. Episodic organizers can be of great use here. First, pupils formulate the ideas that will introduce their essays by writing the introductory topic in an inverted triangle with comments on the topic joined to the triangle by lines. (The upside–down triangle points out the direction to be taken as the essay unfolds.) Next they develop a "con" organizer that represents the point of view in opposition to their own. Then they present the arguments they favor and develop a "pro" organizer. Finally, they draw a conclusion using a right-side-up triangle in which they restate and broaden the major concepts developed in the introduction. This format helps students write a well-organized essay. (See Figure 12–1 and the essay developed from it by a middle school pupil.)

STUDY STRATEGIES

Two approaches to study that appear to be used widely are SQ3R (Survey, Question, Read, Recite, Review), created by Francis P. Robinson,[1] and an adaptation of it—PQRST (Preview, Question, Read, Self-Recite, Test), by Ellen L. Thomas and H. Alan Robinson.[2] These techniques seem valuable when directed by the teacher and when used independently by some students. The authors find, however, that many students use the technique only under direction. They seem to have the greatest difficulty with the Q or question part of each technique.

The adaptation of the techniques here—SQ3R—useful for middle school and junior high school students, substitutes a semantic organizer for the questioning. In place of the R in SQ3R or the S (self-recite) in PQRST, is reorganizing. Instead of the R in SQ3R or the T in PQRST, it is suggested that the student reconstruct the organizer from memory. The initial Survey (or Preview—P) step is retained, as is the Read step. Here are the five steps of our SQ3R with instructions to students:

STEP ONE: S (*Survey*), as rapidly as you can, the entire selection before studying it more carefully. Note the title and subtitles. If there are no subtitles, glance at the first sentences of paragraphs. Read the introductory paragraph(s) and the concluding paragraph(s). When some of the words seem to "pop off" the page, pay attention to them and think about them. These usually are words that are repeated often or are in bold or italicized print. A major purpose of the survey is to get an idea of the major points and how the material is organized.

STEP TWO: O (*Organize*) the ideas gathered from the survey in the same way you felt that the author organized ideas. Develop either a concept or an episodic

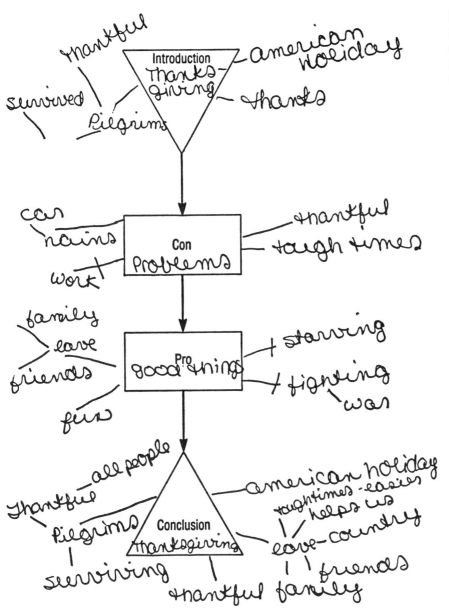

Figure 12–1
Episodic Organizer and Essay It Produced

Figure 12–1
continued

Thanksgiving

Thanksgiving is strictly an American holiday. We give thanks. The Pilgrims were thankful because they lived through the year. They survived.

Some people are not thankful because they have problems. The prices keep going up. Many people have no work. It always rains when my dad washes the car.

Even though some people have problems, there are a lot of things to be thankful about. We are not starving. We are not fighting in a war. Sometimes we can have a lot of fun. We should be thankful that we have family and friends to love us.

It is mostly love that helps us. We love our family and friends and we are learning to love our country. Just like the Pilgrims we and all people have a lot to be thankful for. Not only Americans have a lot to be thankful for but Thanksgiving is strictly an American holiday.

organizer. Don't be overly careful. Even when you are not sure of some of the ideas, write them on the organizer anyway. You can always change your mind later. Right now you can read to find out whether or not you were right.

STEP THREE: R (*Read*) the entire passage in order to add or to change information on your organizer.

STEP FOUR: R (*Reorganize*), using your original organizer if possible. If not, reconstruct a new, more suitable one. For example, if you originally had developed a concept organizer and after reading realized that an episodic organizer would express the ideas better, you will want to develop the episodic organizer. Most of the time, however, you will find that you need only make minor adjustments on your original organizer.

STEP FIVE: R (*Reconstruct*) the organizer from memory. With your organizer out of sight, try to write it again on a blank piece of paper.

Step Five alone can be somewhat useful in studying for a test; however, an adaptation of the entire study plan is best used when studying for a test. There are eight steps to the authors' Test Study plan, which may seem a lot, but they have found its application pays off. In fact, the only complaint heard from students who have used the plan is that they remember so much that they often do not have enough time to write everything they want on an essay examination. The approach is suitable for studying for short-answer as well as essay tests. Here are the eight steps with instructions for students:

Test Study

You can do this by asking your teacher if the test will call for short answers (and if so, what kind) or an essay. Keep in mind, also, the previous types of tests the teacher has given on similar material. Be clear by double-checking with the teacher about the particular material (chapter numbers, notes, etc.) the test will cover.

Step 1: Find Out about the Type of Test

Turn to the topic(s) to be studied for the test. Do not open your book. Think through how much you know already. Develop an organizer based on what you now know *before* reviewing the material in the text.

Step 2: Construct Preorganizer

Preview the text as fast as you can. Note the titles, headings, subtopics, words that ''pop off'' the page, introductory and concluding paragraphs.

Step 3: Survey Text

Add to or make changes in your preorganizer if it is on target. In some cases, you may need to reconstruct it.

Step 4: Reorganize

Now read through all the assigned material without stopping and just as fast as you can. Add to or change your organizer if necessary.

Step 5: Read Fast

If your organizer seems to have some missing parts, look through the material quickly to find the missing information. Rework those parts.

Step 6: Scan for Missed Information

Try to think of the kinds of question that will be asked on a test. Use your organizer to put together answers for essay questions. For a short-answer test, make flashcards based on the information in the organizer, carry them with you, and study them often. One side of the flashcard will be a question you pose, the other side will contain the answer.

Step 7: Study Organizer

One or two hours before the test, reconstruct the organizer from memory. If at all possible, construct it on the chalkboard of the classroom where you will take the test. You will, of course, have to erase it before the test, but you will be surprised during the test how it will appear to be on the chalkboard even though it is not actually there.

Step 8: Reconstruct Organizer Just Before Test

If you cannot do this on the chalkboard, use a blank piece of paper. You can check with your original organizer to be sure you have included everything. Also, think of the questions you posed in relation to the organizer. Do not be shocked if the teacher's questions and yours are dissimilar. Simply pull the organizer back from your memory and select just the items you need to organize for answering the questions.

CONCLUSION   Both concept and episodic organizers are useful in promoting thinking and in developing study strategies. As demonstrated in the chapter, semantic organizers also provide a powerful tool for students to use as they review for a test.

NOTES

1. Francis P. Robinson, *Effective Study* (New York: Harper & Row Publishers, Inc., 1970).
2. Ellen L. Thomas and H. Alan Robinson, *Improving Reading in Every Class: A Sourcebook for Teachers* (Boston: Allyn and Bacon, Inc., 1982).

Chapter 13

Organizers and Lesson Organization

This concluding chapter offers suggestions for using semantic organizers in lesson planning and lesson execution. The opening section, "How Not To Conduct a Lesson," serves as a point of reference for suggestions on lesson planning with semantic organizers.

A teacher had 25 youngsters in a third grade class. Most read on a second or third grade level. On the surface, the lesson described here seems to have many pluses.

The topic of the lesson was Thanksgiving. On the day before the lesson, the teacher had introduced appropriate new vocabulary. Pupils had written words in their notebooks, had looked the words up in a dictionary, and had written definitions.

The teacher opened the lesson by placing a prepared chart on the board describing the story of the first Thanksgiving.

HOW *NOT* TO CONDUCT A LESSON

> The Pilgrims came to America in 1620. They came in a ship. The name of the ship was the Mayflower. They came because they wanted religious freedom. The Mayflower stopped in Massachusetts. The Pilgrims had the first Thanksgiving in America.

Pupils then were asked questions about the passage on the chart:

- When did the Pilgrims come to America?
- Why did the Pilgrims come?
- What was the name of the ship?
- Who were the people?
- Where did the Mayflower stop?

The teacher asked these questions of individual children. If a pupil did not know the answer, the teacher restated the question. If the child still did not know the answer, the teacher gave it and showed where in the passage it could be found. For example, one pupil did not know the answer to the question, "Who were the people?" The teacher pointed to the word "Pilgrims" on the chart and told the pupil that the people were Pilgrims.

After the questioning activity, the teacher gave pieces of paper to three pupils who were reading on the first grade level. These had been prepared with the words "Pilgrims," "Mayflower," and "ocean" at the bottom of each page. The children were asked to draw pictures representing these words.

The other pupils were given an assignment that involved writing in missing words such as the following:

1. The _____ came to America.
2. They came because they wanted _____ .

There were ten such fill-in sentences. The answers were listed at the bottom of the page in mixed order.

The teacher looked at the drawings of the first three children and praised them for their art work. The teacher asked one pupil who had drawn a picture of a girl what the picture was. When the pupil said it was a girl, the teacher told her it was supposed to be a Pilgrim. A boy in the same group did draw a Pilgrim. The teacher told him there should be two Pilgrims and pointed out the "s" at the end of the word "Pilgrims."

The teacher then went to the other group. For the most part, the pupils had filled in appropriate words. The teacher reviewed the correct answers and directed the pupils to change those that were wrong. Before either group could finish the assignment, it was time for lunch.

There are several ways in which this lesson violated basic principles discussed in this book. The first problem was that the teacher failed to establish a cognitive base for the ideas presented. This base must be developed through experience. The pupils certainly appeared to have little understanding of the concepts involved in the lesson. But the most important point is that the teacher did not really have an understanding of how to connect the new information in the lesson to children's experiences or prior information. For the most part, the pupils' only knowledge of Thanksgiving seemed to be related to eating turkey. To begin teaching ideas concerned with the first Thanksgiving, the teacher should have provided many experiences in a variety of ways such as with pictures, film strips, films, or dramatizations in class. The children needed a cognitive base that, in this lesson, is best developed through simulated experiences or the use of focused films or pictures.

Another problem is the manner of presenting vocabulary. Words were presented in isolation and children were required to look them up. Basically, this was a meaningless chore. They needed to learn concepts and vocabulary words in a context, and new words needed to be related to previously developed schemata.

Aside from the obvious waste of time in having pupils draw pictures in order to learn three words, the teacher also ignored the children's need to learn words by relating them functionally to a meaningful context, not simply by associating them with a picture. Only the pupil who knew the meaning of the word could draw the picture, and pupils who did not know the word would have difficulty. This was not a vocabulary learning activity. As far as developing social studies or linguistic skills was concerned, this activity was a waste of time.

The pupil who was corrected for drawing only one Pilgrim seemed to be in the process of being misguided. The youngster apparently had problems related to reading/writing that were more severe than morphological endings of words in isolation. This pupil would have been far better off if the teacher had stressed relationships among words rather than within words.

There are other concerns about this lesson. The teacher told pupils answers without explanation and did not provide sufficient direction in beginning the independent activity. However, the biggest problem became evident in a follow-up conference. The supervisor, who had observed the lesson, asked the teacher to state the purpose for the lesson. The teacher said the objective was to get the pupils to realize that Thanksgiving was not just a day when they ate turkey. In explanation, the teacher said the main purpose was for the children to understand that the Pilgrims came to America in order to obtain religious freedom. However, this "major purpose" was not obvious in the lesson. The teacher had not thought through the relationships involved in such a lesson. A better lesson might have been conducted if the teacher had made use of a semantic organizer.

PLANNING AND CONDUCTING A LESSON

The semantic organizer can help teachers understand the organization of ideas and the relationships of concepts involved in teaching content before presenting the lesson. The teachers need to consider their students' lack of familiarity with those ideas and relationships and plan ways to help students assimilate them. This involves knowing the youngsters, understanding their schemata, their experiences, and their abilities to process information. If the ideas are far beyond the students at this point, the lesson may be inappropriate or the teacher may be able to minimize the gap by providing appropriate readiness activities and experiences.

In the Pilgrim lesson, if it is to be based on religious freedom, the pupils need to become familiar with that concept. First, the concept of freedom should be developed, perhaps through dramatizing and comparing. Pupils can experience the feeling of losing freedom by role playing. After they have some understanding of the general concept of freedom, they can pretend to be Pilgrims in Europe. Role playing might involve their attempting to go to a house of worship and an authority forbidding them.

After the teacher is certain that the children understand this concept as it pertained to the Pilgrims, the actual term "religious freedom" can be introduced. The language needs to be presented after some sort of experience; in this way, it can be assimilated into a previously developed schema. The teacher can help children determine (through play acting) what it might be like not to have religious freedom as compared with having it. The term "religious freedom" should be used often at this point.

The discussion and role playing then can develop into a concern about what people would do if they had no religious freedom. Pupils can be asked to develop their own solutions to the problem. One solution would be to leave the country. The play acting would involve the struggle of packing, departing, and the means of transportation. Further development would involve the trip to America and the joy of a successful voyage.

Based on such background information, the children now are ready to construct a semantic organizer. The organizer in Figure 13–1 helps pupils understand the relationships involved.

Once the pupils have an understanding of the relationships involved, the teacher can vary the assignments depending on language abilities. For some, it may be

Figure 13–1
Semantic
Organizer for
the Pilgrims

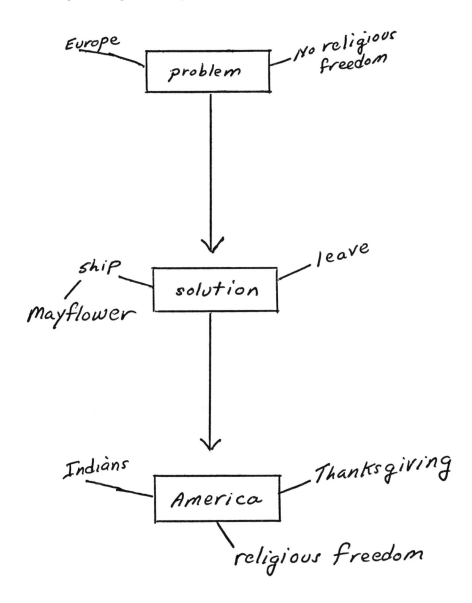

sufficient to copy the semantic organizer into a notebook; for others, it may be appropriate to read a passage that includes ideas presented in the semantic organizer. They then can develop another semantic organizer based on their reading. Some youngsters should be able to develop their own paragraphs based on a semantic organizer.

A lesson should be assessed by the degree of difference it has made in the pupils. New information may be assimilated as a result of a lesson—an expansion of information. However, a pupil also may accommodate previous information as a result of the lesson—a change in previous understandings. A teacher can see both assimilating and accommodating results.

ASSESSING A LESSON

The following example is drawn from an actual lesson in which pupils were able to demonstrate both assimilation and accommodation and the teacher was able to assess this new learning. The objective of the lesson was to teach youngsters to organize ideas related to a topic. They were to read a passage for information about snails.

The teacher had reason to believe that most of the children knew something about snails and wanted to assess their information. A picture of a snail was presented and the pupils were asked to tell what they knew about snails. As each gave some information, the teacher developed a concept organizer on the chalkboard, using all the information they provided and not commenting on its accuracy. The concept organizer in Figure 13–2 was produced from their information.

After developing the concept organizer, the pupils were asked to read the following paragraph:

Snails move slowly but they are very strong. They carry a heavy shell on their backs. They can pull things that weigh more than a pound. They have

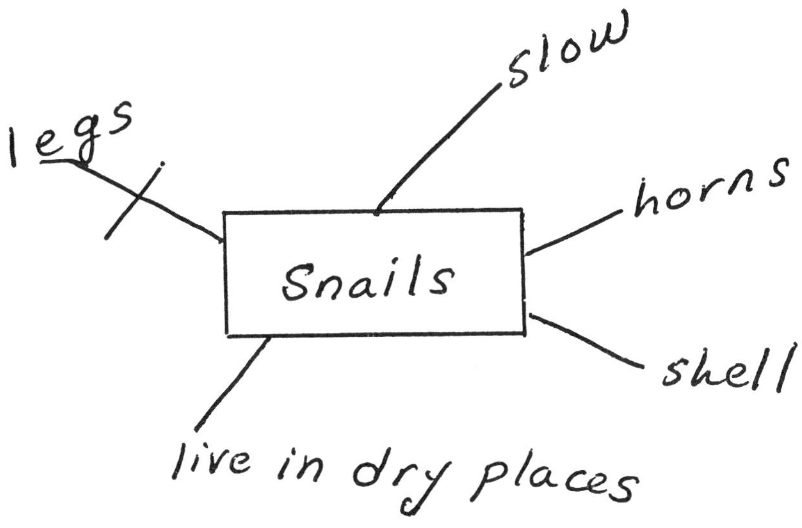

Figure 13–2
Concept Organizer on a Snail

long antennas on their heads and they have eyes at the ends of the antennas. Snails live in wet places. They need a lot of water to live. They like to eat vegetables and so they hurt vegetable gardens. They have many small teeth. Some people like to eat snails.

When they finished the reading, the teacher directed their attention to the concept organizer on the board, asking them to tell what they now knew about snails. Pupils were anxious to add to the concept organizer. The teacher used a different color chalk and added the new comments. The new information represented the assimilation that had taken place.

However, the children also demonstrated accommodation. They directed the teacher to change the word "dry" to "wet," demonstrating that they understood that snails liked wet, not dry, places. They also told the teacher to change the word "horns" to "antennas," which they apparently realized was a more accurate word.

These changes from the previous information represented accommodations the youngsters had learned. The crossed-out words with corrections in the concept organizer in Figure 13–3 represent the accommodations. The underlined words represent the new assimilated information.

Figure 13–3
Accommodation
and
Assimilation

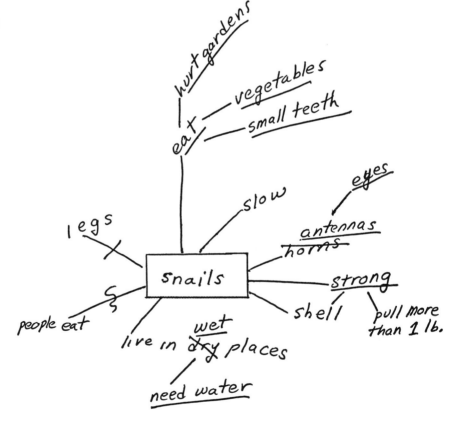

The example demonstrates how a teacher can determine rather easily how much information children possess about a topic before the lesson. New information can be provided as the lesson progresses. The teacher then can evaluate new learning as a result of the degree of assimilation and accommodation represented in the expanded or self-corrected semantic organizer.

Many youngsters who have reading/writing problems also have other language-related difficulties. They may have great difficulty answering questions. The problem is not always that they do not know the answer but that they do not understand the question. Semantic organizers are useful for guiding reading and for developing comprehension strategies during reading. With the organizer, the answers to the teacher's questions can be developed, using simple or basic language relationships with the aid of question marks. This is demonstrated in the next lesson.

DIRECTED-THINKING QUESTIONS

The teacher introduced the topic of volcanoes by asking: "What do you know about volcanoes?" The teacher wrote the word "volcanoes" on the chalkboard and drew a box around it. (The students lived in southeast Idaho and were familiar with the many extinct volcanoes in their region. If they had had no experience, the teacher would have provided a film or other graphic representation.) Billy responded that Mount St. Helens was a volcano. Harry said a volcano "made smoke." Jane said the "stuff that melts and comes down kills people." As the students offered ideas about volcanoes, the teacher constructed an organizer using their own words.

When the pupils ran out of information, the teacher instructed them to skim a short passage in their science books (which had been opened to the appropriate page but turned face down on their desks) and said, "Your comments were very good. You know a lot about volcanoes. Now we need to find out more. I want you to scan the page in your books to find out more about volcanoes. I'll give you 20 seconds (vary time according to children's abilities) to find one or two ideas. When I say 'Stop reading,' turn your books over again. Ready? Go!" The youngsters scanned the text for 20 seconds, when the teacher said, "Stop reading" and they turned over their books.

The teacher asked, "What do you know now about volcanoes?" The teacher wrote the responses on the organizer. (It may be useful to use a different color chalk or a line under these ideas to identify later what children learned from scanning as compared with what they knew before the lesson.) Jane said the "stuff" that melts is called lava. Ryan said the lava temperature is 110 degrees.

The teacher then raised some questions: "Have you ever seen lava?" The students said "on TV." "Yes, but you have seen lava around here, too. When you read this try to think of where you have seen lava." (Remember, this lesson took place in southeast Idaho where lava flows are plentiful.) "Do you know what island has many volcanoes?"

While asking questions, the teacher expanded the organizer by writing key words with question marks after them, then continued the discussion: "I wonder if 110 degrees (centigrade) is hot enough to make lava flow. Please read to find out if that is hot enough. Also try to find out if volcanoes have some good purposes."

Figure 13–4
Organizer
Derived from
Directed
Thinking

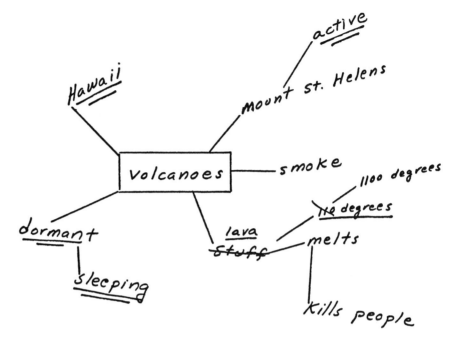

The students then read silently at their own paces. After the reading, the teacher further developed the organizer using a third color chalk (the information could be underlined twice) so this new material could be differentiated from the old. The pupils then were able to answer questions after they read. Ryan corrected his previous error and said, "The lava gets really hot. It gets 1,100 degrees." Marilu said that lava isn't always hot. "It cools off and I saw lots of lava just out of Pocatello. The road is on top (of the lava)." Jennifer said volcanoes that are sleeping are called dormant and Billy said some volcanoes are active like Mount St. Helens. Larry said, "Hawaii is the island that has many volcanoes."

The organizer in Figure 13–4 was constructed during the lesson just described. In this organizer the information pupils gave after scanning is underlined once and the information provided after reading is underlined twice.

After practice with this type of lesson, pupils should be ready to develop their own personal organizers before reading, after scanning, and after reading. They can demonstrate both assimilation (the addition of new information) and accommodation (the changes that took place in their ideas as a result of reading).

**PRE-
STRUC-
TURING
ASSIGN-
MENTS**

In one junior high school, students had difficulty demonstrating comprehension. Their social studies teacher made use of an organizer that worked effectively. The topic of the unit was Japan. The teacher prepared an organizer on a paper for each student. In the center box the word Japan was written and on three legs of the organizer questions were asked in telegraphic language with the aid of question marks. Students used their text to find the answers, then tried to complete the organizer, as shown in Figure 13–5.

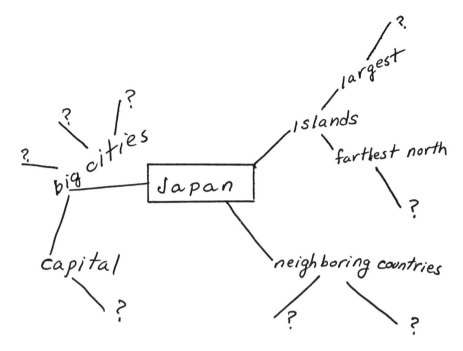

Figure 13–5
A Prestructured
Assignment

Using a similar approach, another teacher conducted a history lesson using a different book for each student since there was a wide range of reading abilities in the class. Each pupil had a book related to the topic of World War II but each book had been carefully selected based on that student's reading ability. The teacher used both the school and the public libraries to collect enough books for the entire class.

The teacher began by showing a film on major events of the war, then asked students to scan through their books and come up with one important fact about the war. Some students had to use the index—a process that had been taught previously. The teacher wrote World War II on the chalkboard and drew a box around it. As students supplied factual information about the war, their words were inserted in telegraphic form. After about ten facts had been written, the teacher asked the pupils to help number them in sequence. After the organizer was constructed and the sequence numbered, the teacher demonstrated, on the chalkboard, how to produce a report based on the organizer, writing out the first five sentences. Students copied the organizer and the beginning of the report from the board. The teacher instructed them to complete the report on their own.

Sometimes teachers need to preteach vocabulary before a lesson because young-sters cannot make use of the context in order to figure out words on their own. Traditional approaches often involve a teacher's asking the children to look up a word in the dictionary or carrying on a discussion of individual, isolated words. Sometimes children are asked to write the words and use them in isolated sentences. These are **PRE-TEACHING VOCABULARY** poor ways of introducing vocabulary. They are boring and largely useless. Children usually fail to transfer vocabulary words learned in this way to functional practices in oral or written language. Vocabulary words taught in isolation tend to stay in isolation. They are not useful for listening, speaking, reading, or writing. Youngsters need to learn words through use in context so the teacher should present words initially in a useful context.

A semantic organizer can be used not only to preteach vocabulary but also to motivate the youngsters. It can be helpful for developing prequestions before reading, thus establishing purposes. It is an excellent tool for reducing the distance between author and reader before reading. Youngsters who have reading problems and become frustrated quickly will need this prior support so they may succeed more easily. By introducing vital, unknown vocabulary words before reading, the teacher can lessen distance and greatly reduce the possibility of the child's becoming frustrated.

The following is a demonstration of how this can be used for preteaching vocabulary and decreasing the distance before reading. In this lesson, pupils were asked to read a story about Thomas Edison. Their teacher discussed the story, used new vocabulary, and at the same time constructed a concept organizer using the new vocabulary.

> Boys and girls, this story is about Thomas Edison who was a prolific inventor. He loved to invent and he invented many things. In fact, he never stopped inventing. He became very famous for inventing things that could run with electricity and that's why his greatest renown was as the father of electricity.
>
> When he was young he was a store proprietor—the boss of the store. As a matter of fact, he was proprietor of two stores. When you read, find out how being a store proprietor helped his future development in becoming a famous, renowned man.
>
> When he wanted to invent things, he needed capital. He always needed capital because without money he couldn't buy the things he needed in order to invent other things. When you read the story, I want you to find out what he did to develop capital. How did he get money?
>
> I also want you to read to find out about the adventure he had with the newspaper he edited. Find out where he ran his newspaper printing press and why he was dispossessed or thrown out of the place.

As the new vocabulary was developed, the teacher preorganized the words on the chalkboard so the youngsters would be very aware of their relationships. The teacher also gave, within a contextual framework, enough information so the youngsters could figure out how to use the words. The vocabulary was pretaught by using the words in the same way they were to be used in the story. Youngsters who would not have been able to read that particular story were able to do so because they were pretaught the information using the concept organizer shown in Figure 13–6.

Figure 13–6
Preteaching
Vocabulary

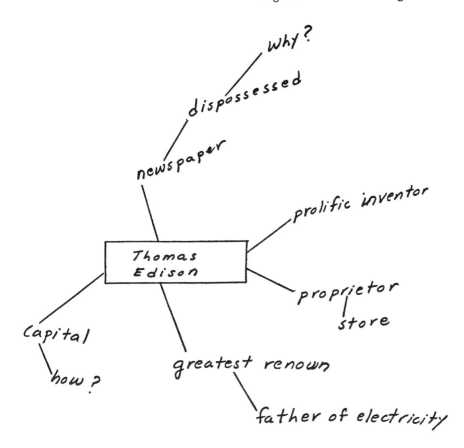

CONCLUSION

In addition to the varied uses of semantic organizers discussed in this book, in this chapter organizers were targeted as aids in lesson planning and lesson execution. They are particularly useful in putting all the pieces together in a unified and connected whole. Both teachers and students view a visible plan that they can modify as appropriate.

The authors hope that what they have presented in earlier chapters as well as in this one will enhance teaching and learning. Obviously, semantic organizers are not *the* one way of teaching. However, they do introduce one important way of tapping cognitive strengths and organizing them for reading, writing, learning, and teaching tasks.

Index

About the Authors

ROBERT S. PEHRSSON is an associate professor in the Department of Education at Idaho State University, Pocatello, Idaho. He also teaches in the Department of Speech Pathology and Audiology there. He taught in the New York public schools (1962-1976) and served as language and reading supervisor at the Lexington School for the Deaf in New York City (1976-1980). His interests are in language development and disabilities as related particularly to the teaching of reading and writing.

H. ALAN ROBINSON is a professor in the Reading Department and director of doctoral programs in reading in the School of Education, Hofstra University, Hempstead, N.Y. He is the author of many books in the field of reading and has served as president of the International Reading Association and president of the National Conference on Research in English. His major interest area is language and cognition, particularly in relation to written discourse.